EYES OPEN EMPLOYMENT

An Owner's Manual
for How to Accelerate Your Career
with Your *Eyes Wide Open™*

BRUCE MIHOK

Allegiant Press

Eyes Open Employment is a work of non-fiction.

bruce@eyesopenemployment.com

831-332-7675

329 Lake Drive

Boulder Creek, CA 95006

"Eyes Open Employment is a definite read for anyone seeking to maximize their career potential or opportunities. The truths and facts about getting ahead in today's increasingly competitive work force have been thoughtfully decoded into an easy to understand framework. This process can be followed in its entirety or can address specific challenges, scenarios or topics. With time at a premium every day the author captures the importance in priorities, execution and becoming the best you can be. Having had the privilege to work with Bruce for years, I have seen his recommendations in action and the true success they bring."

Brad Timchuk
Former CEO
Fuel Industries

"Eyes Open Employment is full of the kind of real-world advice your father would give you — if he were a wildly successful International executive in the Fortune 500. Quite simply, this is the most realistic and useful career training guide that any young professional can pick up today."

Lauren Bailey
President
Factor 8 Performance Training

"Bruce has been first a great boss and then a great friend for over 10 years. Both in professional and personal life, he is one of the most honest and integer professionals (and friends) I have ever met. He lives and acts the way he's suggesting in his book, and was and is very successful doing so. Associating yourself (first Power Point, Chapter 1) with Bruce, if only through this book, is a smart move for anyone at any career level below CEO (and maybe even then)."

Dr. Hinrich Eylers
Associate Provost/Dean
University of Phoenix

"In Eyes Open Employment, Bruce Mihok distills years of business experience into a roadmap of wisdom that will alter one's business success and growth as an individual. He leaves no stone uncovered, laying out perspectives and paths to achievement. This book is a precious gift to the business world and to anyone who wants to thrive within it."

Jeffrie Story
President, Author
Unleash Your Sales DNA

"Eyes Open Employment is a business play book for any age or title. Bruce's knowledge, background, and insight will give you grass roots, ground level direction on how to become a personal champion. A must read for every person entering the workforce or CEO who wants to make a change. When you say you're going to do something, there's always an "out", BUT when you commit, great rewards follow. Professional athletes commit and train all their lives to be the best they can be. This book provides a play-by-play approach on how to become an MVP in business. Are you ready to commit?"

Greg Depinto
Vice President, Sales
SoftWrench Solutions

"Reading through Eyes Open Employment is like seeing in print all the things one has often contemplated putting into words but never did. Mr. Mihok has taken the time to articulate for everyone some basic principles, which when followed would leave the reader on a fast path to a successful and satisfying career. A must read for anyone who is in the working world and trying to find their way to personal and financial success."

Michael A. Kalinowski (Ret)
Sr. Vice President Marketing
SAP, Inc.

"I worked for Bruce when he was Vice President, of Program Management at Direct Alliance as his Program Director for the HP Business Store program. It was one of the most productive and collaborative experiences I have had in a work environment. Bruce is supportive, accountable and is, most importantly, a great coach / mentor. I consider Bruce my mentor to this day. He motivated his team and was always consistent. He thinks out of the box, is an excellent communicator and "gets things done."

Mike Houghton
Vice President, Vertical Solutions
Avnet, Inc.

"Early in my career I had my first management shot. My boss asked me to fill some big shoes…… his. Bruce taught me to organize, develop and motivate an effective sales team. To fight for my customers. Respect and take care of your people. Stand up for what you believe is right but be open to ideas and consider the possibility you could be wrong. Keep an even keel and move forward. He showed me how to give the team space to learn and grow while still keeping things on track. By example he showed the importance of balancing work and family life. His mentorship has been key to my success. Keep your eyes wide open….."

Rick Harder
Senior IT Consultant
Source 1, IT Solutions

CONTENTS

PART ONE:
GET READY FOR THE SPOTLIGHT

CHAPTER ONE:
SUCCESS IS NOT A RANDOM EVENT

CHAPTER TWO:
LET'S GET YOU BRANDED

CHAPTER THREE:
THE BEST OFFENSE STARTS WITH A GOOD DEFENSE

CHAPTER FOUR:
PEOPLE: THE CAUSE OR THE CURE?

CHAPTER FIVE:
YOU AND YOUR MANAGER

PART TWO:
YOU CAN'T PLAY THE GAME IF YOU DON'T KNOW THE RULES

CHAPTER SIX:
EMPLOYERS AS LIVING ORGANISMS

CHAPTER SEVEN:
EMPLOYERS: THE GOOD, BAD, AND THE UGLY

CHAPTER EIGHT:
SHOULD I STAY OR SHOULD I GO?

EPILOGUE

Dedicated to my daughters, Erin and Alexa

INTRODUCTION

Stop what you are doing for a moment. Stop reading this book and put it down. I want you to take a few minutes and focus on your job and think about everything that happens around you while you're at work. Not just what you are paid to do while you're there, but <u>everything</u>. Co-workers, manager, building, company executives, products, financial results, infighting, cliques, the break area, the parking lot … everything! Get out of your ergonomic chair, off the sofa, or push away from your workstation so you're able to take the time to begin to see your world at work with your *Eyes Wide Open™*.

Now that you are engaged, you need to know what to look for so can you understand what you see. You are about to take an objective, reality-based look at what happens within the four walls of the majority of business environments today. This book is the equivalent of the class you should have taken in college to prepare for life in the business world. The only problem is that no college or university offers a class that treats this topic in a totally honest and forthright manner … if anything similar is offered at all.

Eyes Open Employment maps your way through the maze that is modern, self-directed career development. It prompts you to ask the tough questions that require frank answers. Are you aware of what drives the actions of your co-workers, your department, or immediate team? Do you have a good understanding of your organization and its politics, relationships, challenges, and the resulting behaviors that these generate?

Perhaps you may be a bit unclear and find yourself in a situation that is similar to the saying that states, "I don't know what I don't know." Any response to these questions is fine, since there is no right or wrong answer. I understand this and that is why I wrote *Eyes Open Employment*.

Through what you are about to discover on its pages, many of the gaps in your knowledge about life at work will be filled. This is accomplished through a thorough self-examination, as well as a pragmatic look at the environment where you are employed. An inside-to-outside methodology guides you to a deeper understanding of your world. The process begins with a self-appraisal that addresses various topics that assist in the construction of a solid foundation on which to build your future. This is followed by a discussion about managers and co-workers and your interactions with them. An examination of employers delivers insights into the organization that writes your pay check. This opens your eyes to how organizations either help or hinder your ability to make a living and productively progress down your career path. The concept is to look inward in order to learn more about yourself, then outward to determine how to connect with the world around you. You become more able to recognize what you see and, thereby, increase your understanding of what happens around you as you explore in all directions. Consequently, you become better prepared to take appropriate actions when and as they are required. This positions you as a more proactive person and a better informed member of the vast army of people who work for some type of business, government agency, educational institution, or other entity.

Not everything within these pages applies to everyone, but anyone who ever worked for someone else will find much of the content relevant to their situation. Whether you are new to the work environment, in transition from school to work, stuck in a job rut, or in a search for insights into how to more effectively function in the world of business and employment, there is something ahead for you.

During the course of a career that included years of Business-to-Business, Business-to-Consumer, and Government/Education employment, I had both the pleasure and misfortune to interact with a host of individuals who represented a true reflection of our society. Some were extremely positive while others were downright evil. All, however, were enlightening to some degree and provided something from which to learn. At this same time, I participated in a broad spectrum of situations that could be characterized as similar to the people I met along the way—good and bad, positive and negative. What became obvious were the recurring themes that ran through this thread of experience. Year after year, I noticed that many of the things that happened were very close in nature to what I previously experienced. I also noticed that the same type of people with common traits and characteristics were encountered again and again. History did, in fact, repeat itself.

I deduced that if these things happen to me, then they must also happen to others. I knew I couldn't be unique in this respect. Further investigation provided the conclusion that I was indeed not alone in what I encountered on the job. Similar things happen to nearly everyone. The issue that I uncovered during this research is that many of these events take people by surprise, because they are either not prepared, or simply do not possess proper awareness. I cataloged many of these experiences in daily journals and then began to discuss them with numerous business friends and colleagues in order to cross-validate my observations. This permitted the separation of the less common items from the commonplace. The net results of these conversations coupled with my experiences ended up as *Eyes Open Employment*.

The contents aren't limited to what I experienced, but include those of that large group of friends, mentors, associates, and colleagues whom I met along the way. To a person, we all shared a single belief that people who are new to the workplace, employees who want to advance, plus anyone with a desire to improve their personal value to their employer, has the potential to benefit from this book. All of us heard the same questions at one time or another: "How can I get ahead?" or "How can I become a Director or Vice President?" There is no easy roadmap here. These goals are achieved through dedication, the right dose of self-promotion, a keen eye for opportunities, and flawless execution of the basics on a day-to-day basis.

These points are distilled into an easy-to-read format that provides quick reference to a wide variety of useful information. This arms you with the ability to identify and sidestep the same mistakes that others, who do not have access to this knowledge, make over and over again. The contents are useful to anyone who seeks to improve their current position or advance up the career ladder. You will become better prepared to pave your own career path proactively, so that you are able to take advantage of opportunity and mitigate the negatives you encounter. Knowledge provides a sense of security, since you know why and how things happen around you. Ignorance creates fear and a sense of uncertainty and doubt.

The initial outline of my research material indicated that *Eyes Open Employment* should be a book that the reader did not have to read from cover-to-cover. Instead, it became apparent that the material would be most effective if it was organized to cover several main topics, which would then be broken down into related sub-topics. This approach provides a simpler method for the reader to seek and find those items that are of the greatest immediate interest. This also organizes the material into a logical framework for those who want to read *Eyes Open Employment* from front to back.

You may not agree with all that is contained in *Eyes Open Employment*. That is your choice. All of it may not be applicable to your particular situation. That is fine as well, and simply means that you can use the Table of Contents to guide you to the sections that are of most interest to you. My intent was not to provide the deepest coverage on any single item, but to present a wide variety of subjects that you relate to, and as a result, make you explore how they relate to you.

Keep a few things in mind as you journey along your own career path. Certain basics never let you down. You can practice them in any situation with positive results—work hard, be honest, add value, be vigilant and, above all, respect the dignity of all whom you encounter.

This simple phrase is one that I use as a guidepost for interactions with those I meet along the road. It never fails to produce a positive experience, so I share it with you. It will be a point of reference throughout the pages that follow.

PROLOGUE

The realization of success in the business world is a difficult and time intensive undertaking. To the uninitiated and inexperienced, business may seem to be a green field of opportunities that offers reward for all those with an inclination to work hard and diligently apply their skills and knowledge. It appears to be populated with insightful leaders who run companies like the lords of old, expand their footprints, and enrich all of those who pledge their allegiance. It is sold as a world where talented teams of passionate colleagues overcome obstacles to deliver great products to grateful customers and generate ever-increasing rewards.

While all of this may be accurate in some cases, the absolute truth is that today's business world is nothing more than a reflection of our society. It is home to the best and brightest, but in addition, it also provides cover for criminals, cheats, manipulators, and all other less desirable members of our society. Its inhabitants may be sinners or saints and everything in between. While some may call this a cynical view, I believe it is actually an accurate portrayal that gives anyone who adopts it a pragmatic perspective of employment, and offers them the proper measure of protection against the ill effects of wide-eyed optimism.

The unadorned truth is that the modern business landscape is a combination of hard work, unequal rewards, luck, volatile relationships, personal ambitions, passion, plus all the Cardinal Sins wrapped into a work schedule that seldom runs eight hours a day and five days a week. It is a land fraught with unfamiliar situations that cause self-doubt and second guessing. It is a place where logic is often denied and decisions are frequently more emotional than fact based.

Business in the twenty-first century is also a land of true opportunity, when you know how to navigate through its dark and mysterious channels and apply your knack for survival. Those who are short on preparation find they are long on disappointment. Take the time to look around as you progress through this book and decide for yourself what may be applied to your personal situation today. Determine if and how the contents may relate to your own career development. A reference source that meets these criteria is an important asset that can provide benefits over a period of time when leveraged properly.

Remember that business is where fortunes can be made, careers built, families supported, and passion fulfilled. This only happens through careful planning and precise execution. Success is not a happenstance occurrence. When you leave your career in the hands of others or do not have a succinct personal plan, you are in the same category as a boat without a rudder. You progress at the whim of the tide and face surprises around every turn for which you are not prepared to address. Your chance of crashing on the rocks is greatly enhance, while the opportunity to sail blissfully into the sunset is exponentially diminished.

My ultimate desire is to offer the reader a method through which they compress the time it takes to gain experience and achieve increased productivity. A conscious effort is made to provide insightful information that is both truthful and experienced-based. The fact is that, similar to the world outside of business, you can find success, happiness, and satisfaction in your chosen career. Just do it with your eyes open and leave your naiveté at home.

As you read, note that the use of the words "company, employer and organization" should be thought of as interchangeable throughout the book. This is because the majority of examples provided herein are found in all forms of enterprise, including public, private, government, education, and non-profit agencies.

Various sections are expanded through the use of "Power Points." These are relative topics that expand the context of the subject to which they are appended. Together the main subject and the Power Point provide a specific context and additional insights about how you may incorporate both to greater effect.

Finally, at the end of each chapter, there are specific Personal Development Actions designed to bring the chapter contents to life. They provide a simple yet productive means for you to put the words on the page into action. Perform these and you take the next step to becoming an *Eyes Wide Open*™ individual who knows where they are going and how to get there.

PART ONE
GET READY FOR THE SPOTLIGHT

CHAPTER ONE
SUCCESS IS NOT A RANDOM EVENT

It's time to get ready to step into the spotlight. The need to hide in the shadows because you're unsure of what to do when the light shines on you will soon cease to be an issue. It's time to prepare to weave yourself methodically into the fabric of your employer's organization. This ensures that you will receive maximum return for the time you spend on the job, and your employer will realize the greatest return for their investment in you. This is the classic definition of a "win-win" situation. There is no better way to position yourself when your plans include job stability and promotion.

This chapter is about the development of a state of mind that creates your foundation for success. It requires honest introspection. As you move through it, review how you measure up today versus how you will when you become optimized. It offers a framework for behaviors on the job in a way that always lifts you up and never lets you down.

In addition to your daily routine, you face many new, even unimaginable situations during the course of your career. These will never cease to take you by surprise. When you are comfortable and believe you've seen all that there is to be seen, another new, unfamiliar revelation bears its teeth. The secret to handling these successfully is to have a good grasp of basics and a proper mental attitude. These two simple items not only provide the tools needed to deal with day-to-day events, but also the surprises that tend to creep into your life. Many of these present challenges, but solid preparation enables you to manage them so they don't control you.

This chapter addresses how to handle these situations through advance preparation and the adoption of a proactive lifestyle. These basic, actionable methods ensure you become and remain well prepared. They also provide the basic tools to maximize your chances for employment and headed in the right direction.

When taken as a whole, the topics covered in this chapter outline how to lay the groundwork for a state of mind that provides your best opportunities for success. As you read, reflect on the current and desired states of your career as well as your blueprint for achievement. This permits focus on incremental improvements to your current approach that will make you an even more outstanding performer.

BUILD <u>YOUR</u> SUCCESSFUL STATE OF MIND

Your personal brand value

Grooming, speech, work ethic, productivity, clothes, jewelry, etc. all contribute to the sum of your personal brand. Your brand is not just limited to the work you produce or how you act on the job. It is the sum of everything that is associated with you. There has to be consistency in your work product, your dress, personal behavior, and how you otherwise conduct yourself in order to optimize your personal brand. Remember that you are always "on stage" and observed by someone when you are at work. Use this to your advantage through thoughtful projection of how you want to be perceived by others.

Your personal brand has a value similar to that assigned to the good will and brand name of a company. This is known as brand value. Everything associated with you—both the measurable and subjective—create your brand value. Take a moment to reflect on someone at work who either always looks great or the opposite. Maybe they drip jewelry and drape themselves with gaudy clothes that barely qualify as acceptable under the dress code. Alternatively, perhaps they are always fresh and clean with pressed clothes, neat hair, and nails. Do either of these individuals' behavior affect how they are perceived? If both accomplish the identical level of productivity, which one has the greater brand value? Is it fair that we are judged this way? The answer is "No," but fairness is not the topic of our discussion.

Your brand value must be nurtured much the same way that a company protects and extends its brand. The more value you deliver, the more you are worth. It is not an item that can be addressed as an afterthought, since it affects you on a daily basis. Management, co-workers, and customers (internal and/or external) all view you as someone who represents specific qualities much as a nationally recognized product projects their image and brand attributes. Recognize the importance of your brand value. Do what is necessary to improve it through those items that have the most potential to drive it higher. First, though, determine what it is today through a brand audit.

In order to properly perform a brand audit, you must objectively conduct a pragmatic 360 degree review of yourself at work. Determine whether you can honestly calculate your work-related value, your real and perceived contributions, how you are regarded personally, and where you fall in the pecking order of your organization's internal society. If you don't truthfully review your personal brand status and perform an unbiased appraisal, the net result is that you are left to guess about your value and current standing with your employer.

In situations where you are encouraged by your findings, take immediate action to leverage everything that adds value to your brand. Expand your emphasis on the positive aspects in order to take the greatest advantage of your best traits. On the other hand, if your conclusions are less than optimal and the results make you uncomfortable, it is time to take direct steps to remedy the situation and minimize your negatives. Your status is enhanced when you are seen as an individual who recognizes their positive traits as well as their shortcomings, and deals with them in order to improve. This is how to build your brand.

Cultivate your brand much as a successful retailer entices customers through the use of their front window display. Retail stores pay close attention to how they merchandise this display as it sets the tone for what is inside. Ensure you cover the details that create the impression you want to make. Just as the store that does a fantastic job with their street level visual, your brand entices people to want to see what you have to offer. Done properly, it causes people to want to engage with you since it leaves them with a favorable impression provided that your display—your brand—portrays you in a positive light.

Your delivery of timely, high quality work has a major impact on your brand value's appreciation. The production of superior work may appear to be a simple objective, but its execution is not all that common. Look around and take note of how many of your co-workers are known for this trait. You will no doubt notice those who are known for quality output, but also those who deliver mediocre work and earn their place on the lower rungs of the career ladder. That is their brand! Through the execution of your job as a professional, you establish yourself as a "go to" person who can be counted on for both quantity and quality. This is an important light in which to be seen, especially when times are tough, and the company needs to remain lean to be competitive. The projection of this brand trait is also helpful when opportunities for advancement arise. In addition, it is a major factor that commands respect from others both up and down the food chain. Respect = brand value.

That respect is also enhanced when your knowledge base runs both wide and deep. Familiarity about your employer's product line, history, organization structure, and its financial results are some examples of content that should be included in your knowledge base. You should have more than just a passing familiarity with these items, since they affect you and your job. Know who you work for and be able to carry on a conversation in some detail with a stranger, customer, prospect, or a company insider. This type of knowledge displays your interest in your employer, which is a trait that is always well received. When you are in a sales or service position, this knowledge also projects confidence to your prospects and clients, which translates to better, more productive relationships. People buy from people, and prefer to buy from those who are engaged, intelligent, informed, and able to readily answer questions with accurate answers.

Your brand value is also greatly enhanced when you choose to invest in yourself, since your personal growth needs constant attention and nurturing. Learning does not end with a university degree or diploma. Take classes. Read books that are relevant to your job. Increase your value through training and personal development. Constantly look for ways to improve your knowledge base and skills. Find and work with a mentor who has the ability to expand your horizons and who can offer new and exciting ways to think. Network both in and out of your field of interest. Exchange ideas and practices with those in your network in order to arrive at, and remain on the leading edge.

Look around your house and work station in order to do a self-check related to how well engaged you are on this path today. What books do you own that are relevant to your career? Buy and own books that are career builders. Each one of these is an investment in you. Just the fact that you chose to read this book means that you have set yourself apart from others and want to build a more rewarding career.

Every one of these examples is an opportunity to expand your thinking and broaden your horizons. Make a conscious decision to constantly focus on the improvement of your personal brand value. Decide how you can best craft your plan and then diligently work on its execution. Nobody is going to do it for you.

POWER POINT

ASSOCIATE WITH WINNERS

Carefully pick and choose those with whom you associate. Not only are you judged by the company you keep, but often times, the traits of those with whom you associate "rub off" on you as well. You are either elevated or held back by your associates. Both their positive and negative qualities are transferable, so it is necessary to avoid the negative and accentuate the positive.

Are your associates on the rise, in descent, or just muddling along as they journey through life? In general, are they optimistic or pessimistic? Are they whiners, complainers, or are they problem solvers who routinely take action and attack life in order to take advantage of all that it has to offer? This is an area where you have the ability to make thoughtful choices. Know full well that your choice has a considerable impact upon you. It is critical, therefore, that you surround yourself with the best if you want to be the best. Positive associates elevate you just as negative associates bring you down.

How do you "fit" in?

The alignment of your personal culture with that of your employer's is important for both long term job satisfaction and success. This cultural harmony is sometimes referred to as "fit." Fit is nothing more than the measure of how personal and company cultures mesh. This is very subjective, yet tangible. Hiring decisions are often made on the feeling about how someone will fit within an organization. Their skills and experience may be perfect for the job but the decision to hire or not comes down to fit. You may have heard of someone who was passed over for a job because they were not the right fit for the role. This really meant that there was a culture clash.

Personal culture also determines how you are perceived within the organization after you're hired. You must be cognizant of what a company's culture is and also understand that it affects multiple aspects of any job. This is something that truly cannot be known unless you spend time on the job and are exposed to the culture of your employer. An employer's reputation among outsiders is one thing, while what you experience on the job may be completely different.

It's easy for a company representative to state something about their culture during an interview, or to share their Mission Statement or Core Values. Whether or not they live up to those statements is another thing altogether. Too often, well meaning words on a page do not find their way to the day-to-day operation of an organization. Make this value judgment yourself with as little outside interference as possible. Let the written or spoken statement of others about culture be the organization's goal and not their measurement of achievement.

Early in my career, I worked for a fast growing, entrepreneurial company whose culture was one of breakneck pace, innovation, and fast paced evolution. At the time, I was eager, full of ideas, and chameleon-like with respect to my ability to change. The result was high output, great happiness, and rapid career advancement. This was a perfect fit. In another situation early in life, my job with a government agency weighted me down with the anchor of bureaucracy and institutionalized lethargy. As a result, I lived for my payday, hated to get out of bed for work, and performed at less than full capacity. A quick departure for greener pastures made me feel as if I got a reprieve from a long prison sentence when I walked out the door. If the government paid me a salary of five times what I made, it would only have kept me happy until payday, and would have done little to result in longer term happiness. The culture clash was just too great to overcome, and my tenure was short as a result.

A clash of cultures between employer and employee may be disguised by generous compensation or other means, but, in the long run, the erosion of your happiness is sure and steady.

POWER POINT

CONFIDENCE IN YOURSELF

You absolutely must believe in yourself and have faith in the potential of your contributions. Trust your abilities and have confidence in your capacity to execute within the borders of your knowledge, skill, and experience. This mental state enables you to visualize how to succeed at new challenges and projects. This is not to say that you should have false confidence or demonstrate arrogance. On the contrary, confidence translates into how to succeed when opportunity presents itself. This is learned primarily through the understanding of the scope of your capabilities. It also occurs when you avoid those situations wherein you realize your knowledge, skills, and experience will not translate into superior performance. Stick to what you know in the present, but methodically broaden your area of expertise so that you confidently deliver results in an ever-expanding arena.

Confidence that is based upon reality and not dreams is confidence that builds success. It grows gradually over time. As you achieve your goals, your track record does two things: it speaks to others that you are successful, and it gives you self-confidence to reach new heights.

Passion

There are those among us who are truly fortunate because they enjoy their work to the point where they may not actually consider their work to be a job. This is the minority who has found a way to intertwine their passion in life with their job and, consequently, support themselves. When you are fortunate enough to thread your passion with how you pay your bills, you are one giant step closer to happiness and fulfillment. Perhaps the most obvious of those in our society who are examples of this are the successful artists and sports stars who sing songs and play games in exchange for enormous amounts of money. Certainly there is a lot of work and hard labor in their professions, but the fact is that they love what they do and probably would still do it for a fraction of what they actually get paid.

In a perfect world, the pursuit of your passion should include what you do for a living. If you are passionate about clothes, hair, technology, medicine, construction, or any other area of interest, there is a way to leverage your passion in order to pay your bills. Leaving this linkage to chance should not be your course of action. Instead, you should take conscious steps to join the two. Those among us who successfully connect our passion with our work are among the truly fortunate.

We all know what we are passionate about, and our passion provides the opportunity to pursue a career that is linked to it in some way. If you love music but can't sing, your music career should not come to a screeching halt. There are a multitude of associated opportunities in the music field that may be pursued that would allow you to work in the industry. The search for a career that permits you to pursue your passion deserves a concerted effort, and not just for a fleeting moment. This should be something that you pursue for your lifetime, since it really is the path to fulfillment as it relates to your career. You do not want to reach an age where you look back and say, "I wish I had done this or that." Even if you can only chase that dream on a part time basis, you should hold on to it and not let go.

Another thing to consider with regards to passion is that we tend to be good at what we are most passionate about. This provides additional benefits. When you love real estate, you read about it, follow it in the trade publications, keep up to date on line, and stay abreast of the market. This gives you an edge over someone new to the field or who simply thinks it is attractive because there is money to be made. While, in fact, this may be true, the edge belongs to those who love the field and follow their passion.

It is not just about YOU!

Look around yourself at work. Do you see anyone else there? Do you see other people? If your answer is "Yes," then this section is for you. No matter what position you hold, the work that you do while on the job affects those around you. Others are influenced by your productivity, attitude, attendance, and every action attributed to you between the time you arrive at and depart from work. You might call it the Domino Effect: everything you do has an effect on those around you. Your actions cause others to occur which cause even more downstream. Therefore, it is incumbent upon you to do your best, perform at a high level, and deliver to expectations, because everyone affected by your actions depends upon you. Your productivity, in part, allows the organization to hire and retain its employees. Your personal contribution directly affects revenue, margin, and profits. Your ideas for improvement facilitate change that makes your employer more competitive in the marketplace. No matter what role you serve, your impact goes beyond your personal boundaries and affects many others. You do not operate in a bubble, but have a responsibility to act in the company's best interest and in that of your customers and co-workers as well. This contributes to your employer's ability to be competitive in the marketplace, which increases their ability to keep you and your co-workers employed.

Don't choose ignorance

What you don't know can hurt you. This is the reason that life should be a constant learning process. There is a popular axiom that states, "Knowledge is power." It remains as true today as when it was first uttered. Be aware that no matter how old you are or what your station in life may be, you do not know everything you need to know. Accept the fact that you will be surprised and sometime hurt by your lack of knowledge. Consciously work to overcome those gaps through the recognition of what they are and the completion of the necessary work required to overcome them.

This is especially relevant when you are either new to the work force, or to a particular job. It takes months to learn the ropes of an unfamiliar position, so you should be especially vigilant during those first six months in a new position until you learn the processes, people, and infrastructure associated with it. It is a common maxim in business that it takes approximately six months to become proficient in a new role with a new company and nine months to become fully productive. This can vary due to the nature of the work, but it is a good rule of thumb to live by when you find yourself in this position. Do not expect too much too soon from yourself, but consciously attempt to reduce this time through your concerted efforts to build proficiency. Determine what your weak points are and work to overcome them. Seek help, as necessary, from your manager. He or she set your original expectations and you both should be in synch with how your measure up against them at any particular point in time.

Strive for excellence, not perfection

Perfection is a theoretical state. It can't be achieved. If you are a perfectionist, you are also a frustrated individual because nobody ever attains that state. Anybody who puts too much energy towards the achievement of perfection is bound to be disappointed, dismayed, and ultimately fail.

The pursuit of excellence, on the other hand, places you on a path that is both fulfilling and rewarding. Progress towards excellence in your job and other elements of your life is achievable and measurable. You can actually create what is known as a Path to Excellence which is a prescriptive way to access your potential. To do so, categorize the areas of improvement, define how you measure improvement, and put plans in place to increase results in those areas. Then create milestones—identifiable and measureable achievements—that define your progress. Associate projected timelines with your milestones, and you now have a target, timeline, and measurable steps along the way. You now have your personal Path to Excellence.

Perhaps you want to learn a new software program. Set aside thirty minutes a day for three days a week to concentrate on learning and practice. In the course of a month, you will have amassed six hours of dedicated learning. Insert a milestone at the end of the first month that includes knowledge of the program's core functionality, and you have your initial milestone. In a quarter, this expands to eighteen. Insert a second milestone here. Will you be totally proficient? No, you won't, but you will understand the basics, and on your way to a gradual increase in your degree of proficiency. Your personal Path to Excellence for this specific topic is now under construction. Execute the plan and measure your results with a critical eye. You will find that progress will be steady, and many improvements will occur provided you have the discipline required to execute against your plan over time.

Self-improvement is not an overnight event. Permit yourself the luxury of time, so you do not rush toward the finish line only to find yourself disappointed in the result. Be patient. Rushed work is typically of poor quality in self-improvement projects just as it is on the job. Measure yourself over extended periods, such as year-over-year, and you will find you achieved considerable progress provided that you diligently applied yourself in a measured manner throughout this time period.

You may believe that you have a lot of things to learn, but don't overburden yourself with too many items at once. Spread out your objectives over time to permit focus on a limited set of goals. You can become distracted, overwhelmed, and demotivated if you work on more than two or three things at once. Don't unnecessarily challenge yourself in this way. Rather, remain positive about the achievement of a limited set of objectives at any one time. Keep your focus on the quality of your progress, not the quantity.

One of the signs of maturity is the recognition that quality is not rushed. Poor quality work may actually put you farther behind than when you initially began. Shoddy work is a waste of your valuable time, and requires that the original effort be repeated in order for it to be done properly.

POWER POINT

THINK ABOUT THE WORK — NOT THE PRIZE

You may think about the glow that results when you succeed at a task, complete an objective, or achieve a stretch goal. You may imagine how good it feels and the recognition that comes with it. This is what is known as "focus on the prize." Prize focus is a dream-like state that is not a productive use of your time or energy. Dreams about a prize do nothing to complete the work required to achieve it. It is similar to dreaming about that winning lottery ticket.

Your reward comes when your work is executed efficiently, effectively, and on schedule. It should be what energizes you to organize your resources and perform the work. You can't let dreams about what you may accomplish become a distraction that hinders you from the completion of what must be done. When executed properly the first time, your successful labor leads to the achievement of the prize. The reward becomes a reality, and you may then do your victory dance and enjoy the accomplishment of a job well done.

Discipline sets you free

The practice of discipline is an enabler that frees you to deal more readily with those things that are not part of the boiler plate of your life. Discipline allows routine, repetitive tasks to be completed with little or no conscious thought, since you realize they must be done in a certain way on a consistent basis. The result is that these tasks are regularly accomplished with little or no forethought. This is the closest to being automatic that one can be. The opposite of being a disciplined individual is to be either unruly or chaotic. In either of these states, randomness prevails and completion of the mundane becomes something that requires conscious thought and unnecessary effort.

Is the following example a snapshot of you? You get to the office between 7:30 a.m. and 7:45 a.m. because your starting time is 8:00 a.m. This is accomplished because you arrange what you do in the morning to permit you to arrive at this time. Your morning's personal chores are accomplished with little conscious thought, because your sense of discipline has organized them to permit you to accomplish your goal — on time arrival at the office. If this isn't you and you get to the office between 7:59 a.m. and 8:15 a.m., then you have a problem. You may be reading the wrong book. You need to decide if you can import a little discipline into your life, or remain the cause of hours of distress and turmoil for yourself and others for the sake of a few minutes a day.

Discipline, in a broader sense, means you learn the habit of on time attendance for meetings, calls, and appointments. It means job performance that leverages what is known to succeed (standard operating procedures) without an attempt to "re-invent the wheel," unless your use of current practices has first produced top tier results. Discipline means that you learn the basic elements and tasks associated with your job so well that they become second nature and rote.

A co-worker early in my career was exceptionally bright but grossly undisciplined. She was viewed as the Mad Hatter of the engineering department. Multiple, ground breaking ideas sprang from her brain. Very few saw the light of day, however, due to her lack of ability to present them in an organized format that communicated their salient points. Fortunately, her director recognized this as well as her potential value and coached her toward a more disciplined approach toward work. She offered fewer ideas, but those that were proposed were more organized and properly presented. The net was that several of her ideas made it to market and were successful.

Discipline allows you to eliminate randomness and chaos in your personal and work lives. It does not have to equate to your new life as a robot, but rather it means you decide what can or should be executed in a disciplined manner so they become more organized and automatic. It is in this way that you set yourself free.

POWER POINT

YELLOW LEGAL PADS OR JOURNALS

Journals provide a personal history that is gathered day-by-day over time. You may not be aware of it at the time entries are made, but they provide valuable future reference points and pay dividends in many ways. As you begin the discipline of keeping a journal, you should also adopt a consistent methodology for your entries. Include call notes, meeting recaps, phone numbers, names, action items, et al, in a standardized format. The more detailed your entries, the more value you add to this practice.

Journals provide a reference archive that is useful when you want to track down an old phone number, a name you've forgotten, dates linked to specific events, and more. Journals are also a handy reference resource for periodic performance evaluations.

Your notes provide back up and source material about your past accomplishments and contributions.

Journaling also develops a discipline that bleeds over into other parts of your life. When you force yourself into a new, productive practice, it is initially difficult and cumbersome. As you progress, entries become second nature and more automatic. You will find that this process is evolutionary and that it takes less time and conscious effort.

Success is not instant happiness

Happiness and success are not the same thing. Never confuse the two. Someone once said that success is the attainment of what you want while happiness is to want what you get. You can be successful and not happy and vice versa. This is a fundamental tenet that simply cannot be overlooked.

The acceptance of this concept can be traced to your quality of life as well as the degree of happiness that you may attain. There must be a balance between the two, plus a sense of pragmatism as well. While you may want to be successful at work, you also want to live a happy, fulfilled life. Can you have both? The fact is that you can, but this requires a bit of introspection about how you define success and what makes you happy. Do not overlook this internal conversation with yourself. It is vitally important, since these two items greatly influence each other. You must balance your Yin with your Yang, since neither can be fully attained when they are out of balance.

Stories about successful individuals who do not pay attention to their families are perfect examples of the importance of this balance. They are respected by their work peers but reviled by their families. The net is that they lead an unhappy life outside of the workplace. Eventually, this seeps into their performance on the job with an impact that is almost always negative.

There are others, however, who are able to achieve both success and happiness. This usually does not happen by chance but takes a concentrated amount of conscious effort along the way. The guidance here is that while you build your career, also build a foundation for a happy existence that balances life outside of work with what happens on the job.

Reap and Sow

While the adage "You reap what you sow" is a truism for how to live your personal life, it also applies to how you conduct yourself at work. Additionally, this philosophy should not just be limited to interpersonal relationships, but also to how you apply yourself to your job. When you train and educate yourself today, you benefit tomorrow. When you learn new skills, you will reap their benefit at some time in the future. You become better prepared to accept more work, take on additional responsibilities, or move into a new field. When you complete your work with an eye to quality and timeliness, you increase your chances for gain over what can happen if you do the opposite.

The same also holds true in your interpersonal life at work. Respect others' dignity, their work, and the personal side of their life. This provides a much better chance of either personal or professional rewards than if you do otherwise. The same characteristics that make you a good person make you a good employee and co-worker.

When added together, the demonstration of this type of behavior is a major step in your quest to become a higher quality individual, which increases your brand value. These may be high sounding words, but pause for a moment to think about what they mean. Increase your skills and abilities. Treat your co-workers, friends, and associates well. There is nothing much in these statements to object to. Just remember that you should exhibit a degree of patience, and not expect to be immediately rewarded for the seeds you sow. Improve for the sake of improvement. Learn for the sake of learning. The rewards will come. It may not always happen in concert with your plan or schedule, but they come.

A key part of this philosophy is the concept of "giving back." That is, to make an offer to assist others because you are in a position to help and it is the right thing to do. In essence, you give back part of what you receive. This is not a reference to charitable donations, but rather the gift of your time and knowledge to someone who deserves what you have to offer and who respects and uses it accordingly.

Colleagues with whom you may associate may seek advice and coaching from you as you gain status. Some of these individuals are deserving of your time and energy, but others are time sinks. Time sinks are individuals who suck as much of your time as they can under the guise of self-improvement. The downside of these situations is that these people take your time and advice but do not act upon what is offered. In doing so, they squander the value of that which you have to share and ultimately disrespect you. Ensure that when you are asked to mentor or provide guidance that the receiver respects your time, seriously accepts your input, and acts upon the information provided. Your time, information, and experience have great value—do not squander them on someone who is not deserving.

Some individuals seek out the input of others for honest and sincere reasons tied to self-improvement. Others do it because they either read about doing it in a book or seek to ingratiate themselves to the mentor. This is a situation where you, as the mentor, must make a value judgment and possibly just say "No."

Time and energy: non-renewable resources

The elements of time and energy are non-renewable resources. You have a limited quantity of both, so it is incumbent upon you to use them wisely. Much as how you utilize anything to which you have limited access (I.E. money), approach your use of time and energy so that you maximize your personal return on investment.

Time should always be viewed as that which is divided into both work and personal segments. You get paid for your time at work and use that to finance what you do in your personal hours. The goal here is not to confuse the two. Time at work is just that … by real or implied contract with our employer, you are obligated to spend a certain amount of time in the performance of your job. There are, however, limits to the amount of time you should spend at work related tasks. Even though we may be paid for forty hours a week, it is common for many of us to periodically work overtime in order to get important tasks completed. This should not be permitted to become a routine occurrence. Your personal time should be considered sacred, and it should not be given up without thought and consideration. You never get it back once it is forfeited. It should be noted here that the interference of one's job with their personal life (work/life balance issues) is a regular complaint on employee surveys.

Energy is another aspect that must be thoughtfully addressed. In the context of this conversation, "to expend energy" refers to the projection of either positive or negative energy and what you get in return for what you expend. This is not limited to energy spent in the completion of physical acts, but also extends to the impact of energy spent in the non-physical realm.

You have the ability to use the energy provided to you at your discretion. This means that you may use it in either a positive or a negative manner. When you are a positive individual, you expend your energy in a constructive way. This means you use it to benefit yourself and those around you. The end result of your actions is that you focus on the positive aspects of your life that enrich you. This tends to improve the general condition of your environment.

Your energy may also be spent negatively. You can criticize, complain, be demeaning, and otherwise act in a way which is detrimental to your psyche and out of harmony with your environment. When you expend your energy this way, you debit an amount from the allotment that you are provided. The result is that you have a lesser amount of total energy to use and your positive/negative debits and credits are out of balance. This makes it less likely for anything positive to occur and for you to receive the benefits that commonly are experienced when you are upbeat and optimistic. Don't underestimate the value of peace, tranquility, lack of guilt, and other similar positive states of mind.

You channel your energy both consciously and unconsciously. You may wake up feeling poorly. You then attack the day in a negative manner without the awareness that you now emit a very dark aura. Your sullen, aggressive attitude is noticed by others and has an effect on them. It is without fail that this effect is not be beneficial.

Be aware that you have the conscious ability to change this state of mind and make an effort to switch from negative to positive. This changes the way you interact with the world and, ultimately, the way the world interacts with you. When you consciously choose to live a positive life, you take back control, and are not unconsciously ruled by negativity. I believe in the methodology that is summed up quite well in the statement, "Positive energy out equals positive energy in return." Think back to when you were in a good mood and wore a smile. How did the people around you react? The fact is that you have a choice as to how you project yourself to others. This becomes a useful tool when you achieve awareness that you can consciously control this aspect of your persona.

There are times when you find yourself in a situation where you absolutely need a specific outcome to occur. You muster all of your energy into a single, laser focus that essentially "wills" that outcome to occur. You won't take "No" for answer. It is not acceptable. This happened when I was stuck in a blizzard in New York City and had to get home to the West Coast the next day. Flights began to cancel and I had four hours until departure. During that four hour period, I changed my reservation seven times as flights were cancelled and delayed. The net result was that I did, in fact, get out of New York during a thirty minute break in the weather on one of those seven reservations. I flew to a feeder city for my connecting trip home. What made this possible was a singular, positive focus to not become trapped in New York. I willed myself to find flights in whatever airline I could. I walked from gate to gate with my smart phone combing the web for availability. My positive energy was at a boil and my focus was laser-like.

When I got on the flight home, I thought about how many people just gave up and decided to spend the night on the airport floor. I was lucky to get that one flight out but what creates good luck?

READINESS REVIEW

In order to become successful at whatever career you decide to pursue, you first must place yourself in the proper frame of mind. This is foundational. It allows you to align yourself with the course of action that is needed to maximize your chances to advance. With a state of mind that is focused on success, you are prepared to take whatever steps are necessary to advance to the next rung on your personal career ladder. You know your strong and weak points and how to either maximize or minimize their effects. Your attention to a strong mental foundation permits you to build upon it much as how firm footings support the construction of a solid house.

PERSONAL DEVELOPMENT ACTIONS

- List your strongest and weakest areas that relate both to the performance of your current job and to where you want your career to progress. How do these help or hinder you? How can you overcome the weaknesses and maximize your strengths? Create a plan to work on shorter term, quick wins first, and then move on to those items which require longer time frames.

- Write down two or three things that you are sincerely passionate about. They do not have to be work related. What is your passion? Is your career aligned with what you are passionate about and if not, are you actively in pursuit of how the two may potentially align? Happiness is often found when your passion is threaded with your career. Determine if that link is present and how you can tie the two together.

- Track your record for promptness for arriving at work and meeting attendance. Do this for 30 days and determine your natural pattern. Do your habits display discipline and add to your brand value? Would you rather be known as the person who is habitually late or who is always on time? If you are not consistently prompt, determine what the root cause is for your behavior. List what steps you must take to build more discipline into your business life.

- Review your daily notes and determine if they can be used as a reference. Do you keep a daily journal or log that may be referred to for various reasons in the future? Make the maintenance of a journal a part of your work routine. Don't throw away those journals. They may become background material for a book some day.

- Reflect on your state of mind that typically occurs when you wake in the morning and prepare for work. Write down three things that reoccur on a regular basis. Are these healthy, pro-career items or are they the opposite? What are the reasons you chose the answers you noted? If they are not healthy, what can you do to change the conditions that should result in an improved state of mind?

CHAPTER TWO
LET'S GET YOU BRANDED

You are a brand much the same as a Honda car or an Anheuser-Busch beer. You have certain characteristics that make you unique and deliver value. These serve to differentiate you from all of the others around you. The secret here is to know what those characteristics so you may enhance the positive while you reduce the negative.

Brands do much the same in their advertising. They tout their features ("Won't fill you up …") and their benefits ("… so it won't slow you down."). This builds their value and sets them apart from their competitors. The more differentiated value they have, the more they are set apart in the crowded marketplace. This makes consumers more likely to make choices that are favorable to them, and in doing so, drive sales.

Branding is a tool used to identify a product as individualistic in a positive sense, and make it stand out in a crowded room so it is chosen over others. Your goal here is much the same as a company selling their product. You want to be seen as an individual who has unique qualities that positively affect the organization for which you work. When that time for a promotion or raise comes along, you want the choice to be clear … one choice stands clear above all others and that choice is you.

So let's get to work and get you branded!

BACK TO BASICS

Spring training

Why do major league baseball, soccer, and football teams have training camps before their seasons begin? It's because they return to these events every year to review how to execute the basic fundamentals of the game even though they are highly trained and compensated professionals.

Your knowledge of the fundamentals of business, your company, trade, role, and industry are all essential to the execution of your job at the highest level. The more comfortable you become at the execution of fundamentals, the more time and energy you have to spend on those items that occur during your course of work that take dedicated thought and discipline. The basics of your position should be automatic. You should be unconsciously competent with respect to their execution. You must be aware of this and periodically conduct your personal Back to Basics review.

There are six words that comprise the foundation of your Back to Basics exercise. These are: Who, What, Where, When, How, and Why (also known as the "W" questions). These six words never disappoint when they are applied to any situation that needs analysis. They are the basic building blocks of successful analysis. They guide you through an analytical process that leads to a more informed and intelligent view of what is being examined. Your first step, when faced with something that requires examination and subsequent action, is to list these six words with related facts listed as bullet points under each. This enables you to construct a picture of the work at hand, which becomes the backbone of your project plan, response, or conclusion.

Our next fundamental is how to further breakdown and categorize the bullet points you listed under Who, What, Where, When, Why, and How. Most business situations can be assigned to either one of three sub-categories: People, Process, or Infrastructure. When you are in the process of analysis, it is helpful to break down the components of your project into these sub-categories. Most situations, problems, tasks, or initiatives have a "people" aspect since people are involved in all but the most automated situations. "Process" is also common, since it is another word for how people and systems operate and interact. "Infrastructure" refers to the systems, facilities, and the various tools that are used to accomplish work. When put together, these three sub-categories include the majority of items that comprise most analytical projects as well as tactical plans. Provided you followed this methodology, you now have a grasp of the fundamentals of the project, issue, problem, or task that stands in front of you. You returned to the basics, but are still not quite ready to leave training camp and play ball.

Your next step towards the completion of your Back to Basics review is to ingrain a process through which you organize your work and begin to put measurements of progress in place. You must create Action Items. Action Items are specific work packages or tasks that are agreed to and subsequently put into execution mode in the course of a project. Four elements need to be consistently applied to Action Items in order to govern the work, and to ensure that it progresses in a measurable and orderly manner:

- Deliverables: these are outcomes that must be agreed to in order to define the scope of the Action Items. Deliverables are the delineation of the successful outcomes of the work being performed.

- Accountability: this assures that ownership is assigned to the Action Items so that the work is led by identified individuals who are ultimately held accountable for their successful completion and delivery.

- Milestones: these are significant accomplishments, achievements, or check points along the way that measure progress toward identified objectives which support the overall goal of the Action Item or project. Milestones must be aligned to Timelines (see below) so their completion can be scheduled and tracked. This ensures that work progresses per the agreed to plan.

- Timelines: these are the schedules for the achievement of Deliverables and Milestones for the overall Action Item or project. The Timeline is the measuring stick that provides everyone concerned with the work a barometer of its progress. They also specify the exact date of completion.

This completes this exercise, but you are not through with training camp yet. The remainder of this chapter will guide you through your personal review which will prompt you to look inside yourself, so that you may ensure that you are on a solid path forward.

POWERPOINT

KEEP IT SIMPLE

Simple works best. Fewer working parts mean there are fewer things to break. This is true in engineering as it is in process design or any other discipline. Solutions that are too convoluted and complex tend to be the wrong solutions. When you keep things simple, processes that drive success can be more easily replicated and put into motion by a wider scope of individuals. Simplicity reduces specialization which results in fewer people, processes or parts. It also translates into the accomplishment of results faster and more economically by a pool of workers who do not need specialized skills.

Be skeptical whenever you encounter a project or solution that is complex and requires just the right conditions to work properly. Complexity provides too many opportunities for choke points, bottlenecks, and points of failure. Simplicity reduces these and permits a more streamlined approach to any solution. Simple is easier. Simple is cheaper. Simple is faster.

Personal checkpoints

"Don't assume anything" is still a relevant statement. It is true today and will continue to be true tomorrow. It is listed under "Back to Basics" since it is basic to how you must think, work, and consider everything contained within your work environment. You will either be embarrassed or otherwise negatively affected if you make assumptions without first checking your facts. Positive outcomes will be the exception and not the rule.

The avoidance of the negative effects of assumptions can easily be accomplished through self discipline. You simply must catch yourself in the act when you make an assumption, then stop and re-assess your decision making process. This gives you the time plus the mental discipline required to make sound judgments based on fact and not assumptions. You can assume you have the most recent data on which to make a key decision. You can assume the parts you use to assemble the final product have been quality checked. You can assume that a key shipment went out to your best customer as you promised it would. You can assume all of these things and others similar to them, but can you be sure? If your assumptions are wrong, what are the consequences?

This carries over to how you interact with the people around you. Don't be too generous and make assumptions that people will act in positively in response to your positive actions. You will be constantly amazed and astonished by how people act in ways that are different than how you believed they would. If, for example, you are a manager who assigns a key task to a team member for completion before the weekend break, and you assume it will be done before leaving work, you may be unpleasantly surprised Monday morning.

Inspect, measure, calculate

Your grasp of the value of your work and how it contributes to the good of your organization is vital in the creation of your personal value. You absolutely must deliver measurable value in exchange for what you are paid, no matter what area of the business you work in. This is typically measured by sales revenue generated, Key Performance Indicators (KPI's) attained, management objectives (MBO's) achieved, and other similar types of productivity metrics.

At the beginning of the year, companies create strategic plans and cascade them through the organization. As they are passed down from one layer to the next, their attainment is defined by objectives that need to be met. These objectives are usually measured by KPIs or similar metrics that permit the observer to know if the objectives either are or are not achieved. While it is critical to know your objectives and their metrics, it is also critical to know why these are in place, and why they are important to your employer. You should know how they deliver value to the organization, and how they are intertwined with other measures of success.

Start with the measurement of what the organization gained through the completion of your work. Next, determine if any losses were prevented through your efforts. Measure gains related to any process or other improvements to which you contributed. Ask yourself, "What would happen if I do not deliver?" Would the company lose money, not deliver critical services, not earn as much profit, have higher operating expenses, or some other negative impact? Would our customers be negatively impacted and seek to do business elsewhere as a result? When you understand the role you play in the larger picture, you are more able to deliver the value required, instead of being a random worker who mindlessly performs their assigned tasks much like a worker bee.

"Did I pay for myself this week?"

Every Friday before going home for the week, you should ask yourself the question, "Did I pay for myself this week?" If so, how? If not, why not? These are not frivolous questions, but rather very relevant, introspective looks into your contributions that demand honest answers. Companies are measured by results, so it stands to reason that their employees should be measured accordingly.

This can be very useful at review time as well. When you keep a log of your contributions in your journal, you create a compilation of the collected value of your work. In many cases, you are able to attach a monetary value to your efforts, and actually see the offset of your work versus your pay. A major focus of your personal condition of employment should be to pay for yourself. If it isn't, it needs fixed. You need to maintain the equilibrium between your personal debits and credits on your work-related balance sheet. This ensures that you continue to be a valuable asset of the company. Furthermore, it is always better to give more than you receive, since it justifies the continuance of the relationship. This strategy delivers an added value in that it removes a possible negative metric (you cost more than contribute) from consideration at any time you are under review. Just never let it get totally out of balance to the point where you believe the time-for-money tradeoff is not within reason.

The ability to quantify your contributions is central to the creation of a case that you are worth retaining. Be aware that you are always being measured by someone—perhaps by multiple others—and that your employment and possibly consideration for advancement is, at least in part, dependent upon the extent of your contribution.

In order to know if you paid for yourself, you need to know what the cost is to your employer to keep you on their payroll. You are a liability unless you can contribute enough through your work to offset the company's investment in you. You must know what your baseline cost number is. This is not limited to your base salary and bonus or commission, if commissions apply, but must include associated benefits, taxes, 401K contributions, etc. Estimates vary according to exactly what is included in the calculation, but 1.4 to 1.8 times your base salary or average hourly wage seems to be an acceptable range. This means that an employee who earns a $3,000 a month base salary actually costs the employer between $4,200 and $5,400. There is quite a difference between what the employee gets paid and what the employer pays in total. Know your number—or a relatively accurate approximate. Measure yourself against this number. When you do not measure up, take steps to improve your contribution. These data points are very relevant, especially when the economy begins to contract and belts get tightened.

How you pay for yourself varies greatly and depends upon the role you play. This is simple to determine when you are in sales, as your metric is net margin and/or net revenue that you generate. If you are in another role that is less focused on revenue and/or margin, it may be a bit more involved. You may contribute to opportunity generation, process improvement, expense control, product improvement, manufacturing, finance, technology efficiency, or one of many other scenarios. The important point is that you understand the "what and how" and keep a record of your contribution. In situations where you need information in order to obtain this understanding, ask your manager or other appropriate person. Don't be shy. This is always a good conversation to have, since it shows interest and recognition of the company's best interests.

A method used to catalog your contributions is the Weekly Update wherein a template is used which lists major headings for Work in Progress, Completed Work, New Work, Assistance Needed and other categories that may be relevant to your job. First, create a simple template in email or Word format. Fill in this template with your personal data and share with your manager every Friday. You may do this through a face-to-face meeting, email, or phone. Choose what works best in your own work environment. You may combine several Weekly Updates into one if you meet with your manager once a month for a periodic review. This method permits both of you to have a weekly record of your work that memorializes your contributions. Keep this process as simple as possible so as not to be considered a high maintenance employee. It is supposed to be a low time commitment, high return interaction.

Remember, in some positions, opportunities to pay for yourself are not continuous, but are project-based or periodic in nature. This means that you may be able to pay for all or a large part of your personal overhead for an entire year with one major contribution by virtue of participation in a single, significant project.

Once you are comfortable that you understand the basics, your next step is to look around and determine how to extend your value. This can be accomplished through suggestions for improvement. This may include how to streamline process, reduce steps to accomplish tasks, reduce costs, and improved use of automation. Identify the issue, its current state, your suggested solution, and the anticipated outcome/ benefit that could be attained when your suggestion is applied. Ensure that any possible financial implication(s) is or are included. You don't have to be accurate to the penny, but you should suggest a reasonable estimate. This includes investment that may be required or gain that may be realized. Don't forget to include the cost of maintenance after a project is launched or your suggestion otherwise acted upon. Note that the timing of your suggestion should be reviewed in light of the financial health of the company and the current business cycle. It is typically not wise to suggest improvements that require considerable investment during periods of fiscal stress unless the payback is substantial and close to immediate.

Measure progress year-over-year

This is a concept that paints a picture of your personal growth and contributions over an extended time. Measurement of progress over a year eliminates the short term variables that may give you false positives or negatives.

Reflect on your developmental progress over an extended period of time. Do not measure overall progress in short time periods, such as weeks or months. Annual or quarterly periods are preferred to shorter increments as they allow for variations due to seasonality, vacations, holidays, and other vagaries of the business cycle. Those who are slaves to daily or weekly self-measurement often do not see immediate results and become discouraged when their progress is not exponential in these short term snapshots. Of course, your short duration KPIs (such as sales or quality objectives) are how others measure your performance, so these can't be ignored. This section, however, refers to your progress as a business person, in general, and not how you achieve your daily or weekly production goals.

First, you need to know what to measure. This is a good time to review your job description and focus on the core competencies necessary for success in your current role. Next, ensure you know how these are measured. What are the role's KPI's? Another good source of key measurement checkpoints is what your manager discusses with you during your reviews or one-on-one discussions.

Make note of where you were a year ago with respect to these criteria. What is the delta between the performance level today versus last year? What is your skill level relative to what you need to be successful? Do you close a higher percentage of sales, or have a better record of accuracy, quality, or other KPI? These self checks provide insight into how multiple incremental improvements made on a regular basis add up over a year. Of course, this is easier when you keep your activities log in your journal up to date and complete your Weekly Updates on a regular basis.

Give yourself a chance to succeed. Don't beat yourself up by self-analysis performed over too short a time frame. It causes unneeded anxiety, and offers little value. Do, however, methodically log your activities in order to create your personal track record. This prepares you for your next step because it highlights your strong and weak points. It also illustrates the areas on which to focus so you eventually become the best that you can be.

POWERPOINT

BE MOTIVATED BY SETBACKS

We all hate to lose, and we especially hate to lose at work. The point to understand here is that nobody is perfect. These imperfections, and the environment within which we work, can lead to setbacks. These can be handled in several ways: dwell on the failure and be miserable, or review the events that led up to the failure with a critical eye and leverage this as an improvement opportunity. Setbacks are a natural part of life. You make a better impression by how well you recover rather than how badly you failed—provided that you use the setback for self-motivation and plan your counterattack quickly and intelligently.

It may seem trite but the expression, "Learn from your mistakes" is actually very true. A misstep is typically the result of a decision that was made. When a setback occurred as a result, then your decision was either incorrect or its execution was flawed. Either way, the result offers an opportunity to review the process and learn from root cause analysis. Review, improve, and if possible, make another decision which takes the new information into account. Rinse and repeat, if necessary.

Communicate in the positive

The vast majority of topics we communicate should be done so positively. While this may seem to be one of those sayings that make you say, "Sure, I know that," the meaning of this is quite profound. It is also a concept that is totally overlooked by the majority. Consciously review how you speak and write over a two to three day period. Do you use a great many negatives? Do you refer to the downside potential of the topics and not the upside? Do you frame your communications negatively when they could be offered in a positive manner?

When you write, proof read your material, and look for words such as "not, never, no, without, if, and can't." Determine if the same thought could be communicated positively when you see these words in written form or hear them spoken. This is similar to the glass half empty, glass half full analogy. Practice how to re-word your communications in order to make them reflect a more positive outlook.

A good place to begin to do this is with email. Emails are typically short and do not require a lot of effort to review and edit. I re-read all of my emails before I hit the "Send" key to this day. This often results in the need to re-phrase statements in order to give them a positive instead of a negative context. Taken by itself, this is nothing major, but since you seek small, incremental ways to improve, it is important and it reinforces many other ways to take other small steps forward. You appear more committed, stronger in purpose, and constructive to the receiver of your message when you communicate in the positive.

Another example of how to learn positive, powerful communication is through the use of the phrases "I believe" or "I will" instead of "I think" or "I may." This should be done both in your writing and speech. "I think" is an excuse to fail, not to deliver, complete a task, or otherwise succeed. If you "think" that your answer to the question is correct, are you convinced that it truly is? Does someone who listens to you feel convinced as well? They probably don't. The use of the word "think" in speech and written form weakens your communication and detracts from the strength of your position.

When someone tells you they "think" they can deliver their project in five working days, what have they really said? The truth behind the statement is that they are not convinced they will succeed, and that their use of "think" provides an excuse to fail. If someone thinks they will come to a party at your house, do you believe they will actually be there? Don't count on it. Set the table for one less. If they really wanted to commit to attend your party, you would have heard "Of course." The fact is that they are already searching for ways to avoid your party.

This is a very easy practice to observe, since nearly everyone uses this verbal and written crutch. People in all stations of life constantly think they can do this or think they can do that, when in reality their use of "think" is nothing more than preparation for their pending failure. Listen to political speeches, executive presentations, and even normal conversations that happen around you. You will be surprised at how often the "I think" crutch props up weak commitments or points of view that are not committed to by the speaker. When you want to appear strong, use "I will" or "I believe." Express commitment in your speech and writing, so you are perceived as a person with a demonstrable point of view instead of one of the wishy-washy majority.

POWERPOINT

TAKE THE "I" OUT

Review the last email you just wrote—how many times did you use the word "I" in it? In order not to appear to be self-centered, learn how to write business correspondence with the minimal use of "I". This practice paints you as more team oriented, approachable, and less self-centered.

Your removal of the word "I" from your written and spoken communication is a much more powerful way to communicate than your repeated use of this pronoun. Review your email, letters, and speech for how often you use it. I personally was surprised at how frequently this expression of self was used until it was pointed out to me earlier in my career. As soon as this happened, a personal campaign was launched to drastically reduce my dependence on this word. To this day, correspondence and speech are always checked to reduce the occurrence of this word.

You may form sentences and not have to resort to the use of the "I" word. Start with your emails to colleagues. Review them before they are sent, and restructure sentences in a way that reduces dependence upon this word.

Become a skilled presenter

Possess the skill of public speaking and you become more comfortable in both one-on-one and group settings. These skills are transferrable between large and small groups. It should also be noted that this includes conference calls over the telephone or via video conference. Your comfort with speaking is vital if you are to gain others' confidence. It also conveys a feeling of trust and believability. This skill is not just limited to classically defined sales situations, but includes all instances wherein you interact with someone in a business situation. It should be remembered that you constantly sell yourself in the business world. Everything you do within the four walls of your own organization is a sales effort. Don't kid yourself and think that selling only occurs in front of a customer. When you review your performance with your manager, you are in a sales situation with yourself as the product. In situations where you make a suggestion to a change in a procedure, you sell yourself and your idea. Everything you do sells your most important product—you—and the best sales people are always the best at delivering quality presentations.

One way to gain the skills you need is to take classes, attend seminars, and join an organization such as Toastmasters. This investment in your personal skills pays dividends for a lifetime. The earlier you dedicate yourself to this self-improvement choice, the more dividends you receive as your career progresses.

I worked with a Facilities manager who was engaging with friends, but very shy and retiring with groups and strangers. I encouraged her to join Toastmasters to help her overcome this gap. After a couple of meetings, she made the commitment to fully pursue every benefit the organization had to offer. This dedication provided her with opportunities to lead discussion groups, present to various audiences, and give the occasional topical speech to a large group. These events changed her life because they allowed her to become more confident in all situations. This confidence permitted her the freedom to concentrate on the content of her presentations, since delivery no longer intimidated her. My payback was when I watched her deliver a successful talk to a large group of her professional peers while on stage at an industry gathering. This previously would have been unthinkable had she not consciously made the effort to overcome her fears.

Don't stop with the spoken word, though. The written word and the use of presentation tools are also vital in your journey toward professionalism. Written communication is a window into your education, intelligence, and the scope of your knowledge. Think about the last time you received an ill written letter or email, and what your reaction was when you read it. Communication through the written word as well as through the utilization of tools such as PowerPoint can be either a credit or a debit. It depends upon how you execute, since the power of the written word can be a two edged sword. A well crafted note, email, or paper can project a positive image that increases your value in the eyes of the reader. The opposite is also true, and the results are instant and lasting. One typographical error, grammar mistake, or incorrectly spelled word has the potential to do damage beyond what you might expect.

Take the time to do some self-analysis on this topic. You may want to create a writing sample to share with a trusted friend or colleague in order to get their feedback. You may want to receive constructive feedback from that same individual on PowerPoint presentations that you previously created. These examples provide a measurement of where you are today, so that you set the benchmark against which your future progress will be measured.

POWERPOINT

NEVER TALK "TO" ANYONE

When you talk "to" someone rather than "with" them, the conversation becomes framed as a superior addressing a subordinate—senior to junior. Nobody likes to be talked "to." Everyone prefers to be spoken "with." Think about how you left your last conversation with a colleague. Did you say, "I'll talk to you tomorrow" or "I'll talk with you tomorrow?" The difference is subtle and subliminal. The conscious decision to change your speech patterns in this manner translates into a more respectful relationship with others. Their responses tend to be more positive in return.

Since you do not want to appear arrogant, it is a good practice to remove this from your speech pattern. One exercise that works well is to observe the prevalence of this practice in everyday speech. Listen to others' speech patterns. You will undoubtedly hear "talk to you" or "speak to you" more often that the preferred alternative.

Meeting protocol

Meetings are opportunities to market yourself because you are in front of multiple co-workers at one time. Meetings should be viewed as both business and social gatherings. They have a business purpose, since that is the basic reason they occur. They also bring people together so, therefore, they have a social element. Don't forget these two simple facts when you lead or attend meetings. And don't let the social overtake the business aspect.

When you attend a meeting that you personally organize, arrive early and sit at the head of the table where seating arrangements make this possible. When it is not your meeting, do not sit at the head. This is a position of power and should be reserved for the organizer or a senior invited guest. When seating is at a round table, face the door so you can monitor traffic in and out of the room. When it is your meeting, you must act like it's yours, and not defer to others with respect to seating, even if they outrank you.

Always start on time and end early. Never recap meeting progress for attendees who are tardy. Once started, proceed as if the interruption caused by a late attendee did not happen. When you stop and restart, the meeting's flow is interrupted and control is transferred from you to them. Their late arrival is a signal that they consider their time more valuable than yours, so treat them accordingly.

Meetings should have a clear purpose with just a few simple guidelines. Make sure each has an Agenda as well as Next Steps, Next Step Owners, and Timelines. These are the basics of each and every meeting that you sponsor and lead. It should also be the expectation you have of others for every meeting you attend. A meeting without an agenda is like a ship without a rudder. It may never get to where it was originally headed, but instead wander aimlessly without making true progress.

You typically should first make brief introductions, but only as necessary. Next, cover Old Business, which has been carried over from previous meetings (if applicable). Call on Action Item owners to provide recaps as required, keep it simple, and move through the agenda while acting as facilitator.

Next, address New Business, which are new agenda items that relate to the basic topic the meeting.

All meetings should not end until Next Steps, Timelines, and Deliverables are clearly defined and assigned. This simple discipline ensures that your meeting has an agreed to outcome. Your result will be more consistent and productive when you keep this simple concept in mind as you construct your meeting agendas. These three items should also be included in follow-up notes sent to attendees and invitees. Send the meeting notes as soon as possible after it concludes. Finally, just because a meeting is scheduled for sixty minutes, it does not have to last for sixty minutes. Respect others' time and finish early when possible.

Since meetings are about people as well as business, ensure that your social skills are proper. Remember that you build your personal brand through your actions. Maintain the balance between the social and business aspects of the meeting, especially if there are attendees who are new or who have not seen each other for an extended period. Provide time for short introductions and minimal social chatter. However, be prepared to cut this aspect short whenever it begins to become excessive.

Opportunities frequently occur to advance your brand when you attend meetings that you do not host. Choose to be an impactful attendee. Ensure that you always arrive prepared. Accomplish this through the review of materials ahead of time. Know the agenda items that are to be discussed. Have your suggestions and questions prepared for presentation. Say something intelligent and impactful, but not contrived, at every meeting you attend. This leaves a lasting impression on those with whom you just interacted. Silence is always a good alternative to babble when you don't have such a comment.

Ensure that you extract maximum value from attendance through participation in the discussion relative to covered materials, but also by virtue of your general conduct. Do not catch up on email, text on your mobile phone, or daydream. Most importantly, do not fail to add value to the proceedings by being a silent, non-contributor. You are invited to meetings because your input is considered valuable, so ensure you do not disappoint. These are sure ways to impact your personal brand and your perception as a professional by others. Use meetings as tools to consciously add to your value.

Bad news is like spoiled fish

The old adage is "Bad news gets worse with age, just like spoiled fish." People expect bad news—it is a part of life. Whether it is in the realm of personal or professional experience, bad news is always be part of the landscape. Keep this truism in mind when you deal with your manager, customers, and others with whom you interact. The point to remember is that the earlier someone knows about negative news, the quicker they can begin work on steps to mitigate its effects. They can place contingency plans into effect, deploy resources, adjust timelines, and other courses of action designed to lessen the damage. When they lack knowledge about the presence of bad news, it means they maintain the status quo as if nothing unforeseen is on the horizon. The ultimate, ugly scenario occurs when the bad news is uncovered and it is a surprise to everybody but you. Your credibility immediately evaporates. The assumption is that you previously knew about the issue, but you chose to hide the information. Those affected by what is now a debacle lose the opportunity to mitigate any ill effects. They lose time, money, good will, and your reputation suffers irreparable damage. Proactively communicate the bad as well as the good and you differentiate yourself from the crowd.

Whether you deal with your manager, colleague, a client, or someone in your personal life, it is improper to withhold bad news simply because it makes you uncomfortable. This only serves to makes matters worse. The most productive strategy is to share the news as soon as possible, work with the receiver on damage control, then take corrective action to prevent similar occurrences in the future. Many businesses recognize that negative events will occur in their organizations. They have Corrective Action Plans (also known as CAPs) which identify the issue, its root cause, and actions that must be taken to remediate the damage in order to ensure it will not occur again.

When you work with a client and your bad news affects the delivery of their order, for example, you must let them know as soon as possible about delays without being asked for an update. They may be upset about the negative information, but will ultimately respect you because you informed them and did not have to be asked. This permits them to plan and take appropriate actions. If, on the other hand, you withhold the information because this type of information makes you uneasy when it is shared, your customer will not only be upset about the news, but will lose trust and respect for you and your organization.

Don't press "Send" so fast!

The first person to respond to an important internal email that is shared with a group gains them nothing. Being first, in this case, has no value. The initial respondent may answer from a position that is passion-based, not well conceived, and illogical. Take your time to read the original note, and then determine what request it contains and response it demands. It is helpful to underline the main points of the email so that you do not miss anything important. This also allows you to create a point-by-point answer. Give yourself the luxury of viewing a couple of the initial responses offered by others. The opportunity to see how your peers respond to important issues or questions is lost when you respond first. You also lose the ability to re-assess your perspective if you immediately respond to a group communication. The differing points of view which may be presented by early responders could prompt you to change your original thoughts based upon new information they contain.

Gauge the temperature or position of your co-workers by their responses. Are they informed, misinformed, hot, cold, or otherwise? When you take your place in line and not rush to the front, you can learn from others in the short term, and possibly make a contribution heretofore unforeseen. This may also provide an opportunity to avoid a personal embarrassment through the leverage of insight that you did not previously consider. This is not an excuse to waffle, be tardy in your response, or not have a point of view. On the contrary, it allows you to be better prepared in support of your point of view, since it offers you insight into the thoughts of others. It is very necessary to be timely in your responses, but it is more important to be accurate in the portrayal of your viewpoint than to be first in line.

As you reach the point when you know what your response is, make a pledge never to send a first draft of anything. Match the message to the need and ensure that your communication is appropriate, well written, and correctly formatted with respect to spelling and grammar. You are judged by how well you communicate, so it is vital to proof read everything you send as it carries your personal brand.

I have seen co-workers become embarrassed and even humiliated when they failed to proof read their work. Words that can pass spell check may sometimes come back to haunt you. This is common with some profanity. Misspelled names are also among the worst offenders. Some names which are uncommon to those of us in the Western world can easily be spelled incorrectly. This in itself is unfortunate, as it may be considered as a sign of disrespect. This causes additional issues when the misspelled name resembles a Western word that should not be used in the workplace.

Another point that may seem minor but has the potential for disaster is the use of improper "Send to" addresses for your email or internal Instant Messages. Never be in too big of a hurry to not double check your "Send to" addresses. The wrong item sent to the wrong person can kill a career within an organization. Your reputation must be protected. Years of hard work and effort can evaporate in an instant when the wrong message gets sent to the wrong person. This is something that can be learned quickly with practice. Ensure that before you send your communication that you simply include a double check of the recipient's name as the first item in your re-read process. This will become ingrained within a short period of time, and result in an additional layer of protection between you and a clumsy, inadvertent mistake.

An improper email sent to the wrong receiver can cause more than its share of issues, but other communications can also come back to haunt you mercilessly. You can't be careful enough how you communicate and to whom you send messages. A good piece of guidance to follow is that if you don't want it read aloud in public, don't send it.

During my career, there have been less than a handful of co-workers with whom I have trusted confidential information. I make it a practice to keep all sensitive materials private and confidential. This usually means that I do not share it with anyone. The reason is simple; people who demonstrated to you that they were trustworthy in the past sometimes undergo a change of character without warning.

A global colleague we will call Sanjit spent eighteen months in the Asia Pacific region in an operations role. During his tenure there, he earned the respect of several highly placed executives through hard work, diligence, and his excellent knowledge of the business. They shared confidential information with him so that he could offer feedback and opinions. In short, the region's executives learned to trust Sanjit over time. He, in turn, trusted his boss with select information that he believed his boss needed to know in order to effectively execute his role as a Vice President. It must be mentioned that the regions did not particularly welcome global employees, so my colleague's position was a very positive anomaly. The walls crashed down when Sanjit was trusted with some rather delicate information that he felt compelled to share with his boss. He sent a note to him with the caveat that its contents needed to remain private between the two of them. His boss ruined all of the relationships that Sanjit had meticulously constructed in Asia Pacific when he shared Sanjit's email to multiple others without his permission and knowledge. This was in direct conflict with the request for confidentiality from the regional executives. The leak immediately got back to the Asia Pacific leaders, and Sanjit was essentially black-balled from further contact with anyone of any stature in that part of the world. He was ultimately recalled back to the United States and reassigned because he became ineffective in his previous region.

Sanjit's mistake was that he had confidence in someone who, for some unknown reason, felt that it was permissible to violate that trust without warning. What his previously trusted Vice President would not think to share in the past was made public without notice. Because his boss carried an executive title did not mean that he had status as an honorable individual.

Place yourself in this same situation. You need to run your business with your head out of the clouds, and focus on how to prevent yourself from self-inflicted injury in situations such as this. This type of damage causes issues from which you may never recover. Your first measure of defense is to determine exactly what you believe should be shared. When it comes to the maintenance of confidentiality, nothing beats keeping the information to yourself. There is a large gap between being trusting and ignorant. Trust the wrong person with a confidential piece of information, and you cross that gap very quickly. Once that gap is crossed, the action can never be undone.

If you don't want something to be made public, don't write it down. The written word has many avenues that take it to the public eye. In Sanjit's case, he could have called his boss, but instead he chose email. That may not have prevented the executive double cross all together, but it would have prevented his Private and Confidential email from its transformation into a public document.

POWERPOINT

USE YOUR SUBJECT LINE WISELY ON EMAILS

Subject lines are separated into two types: those that leave the reader with the word "Huh?" on the tip of their tongue, and those who prompt the reader to think "I get their message. It's about ... ."

Busy people develop techniques to scan their Inbox efficiently in order to save time. One of the most popular methods is to scan Subject lines as to the whether or not emails are relevant. Since you want your email to be read and not deleted, it is imperative to develop a skill that enables you to write brief and impactful Subject lines.

Descriptive Subject lines also permit emails to be filed efficiently for future reference. Crisp, relevant Subjects make the retrieval of emails in the future much easier for the recipient.

Examples of what you might use in various situations are: reference to a meeting with the date and possible action item ("Subject: Project X Meeting, 6/22: data quality"); a phone conversation with its date and topic ("Subject: Our phone conversation, 6/22 RE: data quality); a specific question you were asked to personally respond to ("Subject: Your inquiry about data quality, 6/22").

SEVEN THINGS NOBODY ELSE WILL TELL YOU

Become a customer advocate

Sadly, many businesses and their employees do not place enough emphasis on their internal and external customers. They focus instead on profits, revenue generation, and the completion of their work, but often never enough on their customers' satisfaction. Their emphasis is on selling <u>to</u> prospects instead of getting prospects to buy <u>from</u> them. The difference between the two is enormous. "Selling to" places your company in vending machine status. The customer places coins in the vending machine and out pops a product that is more often than not used one time and then discarded. "Buying from" places the choice of how the business transaction is conducted in the customer's hands and makes you more of a partner in the transaction. This inherently leads to more follow-up purchases and a more productive relationship for all concerned. The same point of view is valid for internal customers as well. Those who are involved in what the final work product is and how it is shaped and delivered are bound to be happier and the resulting relationship more rewarding.

When you become a customer advocate, several important things happen. A satisfied customer, whether internal or external, becomes and remains loyal to you. They are always on the lookout for some-one who treats them respectfully, and when they find that respect, they tend to be faithful. Internal and external customers both relish this level of attention. They need to always be considered as business partners and not transactional customers. Commercial accounts, when treated properly, use your services or buy from you repeatedly. These secondary, follow-on sales are cheaper, since the acquisition expense related to their first time buy does not have to be factored into the cost of sale. This is the path that enlightened organizations tread when they build their business. They realize that there is much more value if they become a trusted partner with their customers rather than being a coin operated device. You should be aware of how your organization treats its customers as this behavior is the true embodiment of its core values in action.

Customer advocacy goes beyond sales, though. Each of us has cus-tomers for our work output. You need to be cognizant of their degree of satisfaction. The recognition of this fact brings what was previously said about how your company treats its customers down to the individ-ual contributor level. Internal customer satisfaction is a good indicator of synergy in the workplace. It shows that the employees respect each other. It acknowledges that teamwork is critical to the viability of the organization. The satisfaction of internal customers goes a long way in both the prevention and elimination of dysfunction in an organization.

Higher levels of internal customer satisfaction typically increase external customer satisfaction as well, since the halo effect of what happens inside is transferred to the external customer base.

Budget knowledge gets you in the game

Are you aware of your department's budget allocation year over year? What was its spend last year? Is it flat quarter-over-quarter, or will it be reduced due to budgetary constraints? Get to know your department's budget, forecasted results, and how these affect you and your work within the current and upcoming quarters. When you have the knowledge of these and other similar financial-related items, you can interpret many of the actions and decisions that occur around you. Knowledge enables those things which are unclear to become more focused. This allows you to be action-based and prepared to take measures that enable you to either protect yourself (when the knowledge indicates negative signs), or project yourself (when the knowledge indicates opportunity is at hand). Do not be a mindless bystander, but become engaged in those areas of the business that affect you.

How is your department's budget broken down into its component parts? What portion is dedicated to projects, capital spending, travel, etc.? What is the area or line item that is most under the microscope by management? Do not be afraid to ask questions of those who may know, since this data does have an effect on you. Armed with knowledge, you can become an advocate of programs that have the potential to make the organization more successful. Without knowledge, you are in a reactive mode which gives you little choice, less power, and relegates you to the status of a pawn in the game.

Understand what projects and programs will be funded, and expectations for their delivery. What is the plan in place to extract value from any investment? Is it the right plan? How can you add to the plan? What is your part or your group's part in it? If you are not included in the budget and forecast planning and review, should you be and if so, what should your personal role be?

POWER POINT

BE COMPETITIVE

Competition keeps you sharp, at the ready, and at the top of your game. It provides the edge you need to win. You tend to perform at a higher level when you have something at stake.

I led a generally lackluster, complacent group of telephone sales agents at a global manufacturing company. Our product was superior and priced right, but the sales teams reached a comfort level in pay. As a result, sales' performance hit a plateau then leveled out. I decided to hold a contest to get the competitive juices flowing again.

We bought an authentic, signed team jersey from our local pro football team and built a sales contest around it. Nearly everyone responded positively to the competition. It didn't matter if they liked football or not. Everyone got in the game. Sales literally shot up from the first day and continued to climb throughout the contest. The shirt became a symbolic trophy for the winner who excitedly waved it in the faces of his competition. The moral is quite simple here: competition stirs something in us and raises our performance.

There are alternatives for those who are not prone to public displays of competitive spirit. You may choose to compete overtly on the job, but you can also do so on a more private level. Competition within yourself to attain your personal goals is one method. Competition with a single colleague or friend is another. It is always healthy to have something at stake that provides the drive to accomplish and succeed. Always make it a habit to decide what your competitive focus is, and let it add to your drive to excel.

Funding: Don't start your trip without gas in the tank

Another example of how assumptions have the potential to place you between a rock and a very hard place is the assumption that a project has approved funding without assurance that this is indeed true. The creation of a project without funding approval is organizational insanity, yet it seems to happen all too often. Always get funding approved before a project begins, since budget is the engine of a project. Without it, projects have no life, and can't proceed toward fruition. A project plan may be in place, a team assembled, and work may even begin but without budget for execution, all of this is a waste of time and energy that could be applied more productively in other areas. It is probably also against organizational policy.

An associated point is to ensure your funding is secured in writing before work commences. Oral budget promises, even when made by a CEO or other senior exec, are hollow, even if they are made with good intentions. Your CFO or controller can simply deny a request for budget based upon some spoken promise for numerous reasons. The result is that your work stops. Your project may not appear to get off the ground and in execution mode as quickly as you might prefer when you use this methodology, but in the end, it is quicker and more efficient. When budget is approved prior to launch, you are assured the tools that are necessary to finish the work are in place. Actually, the budget approval step should be included as a key part of your project plan in order to bake it into the milestones and timeline. The practice of not starting a project before funding is assured also keeps you out of "corporate jail." Corporate jail is a reference to the trouble you find yourself enmeshed in due to the initialization of a project without budget approval. This is the same thing, in many organizations, as the misappropriation of resources and the consequences can be dire. This can range from embarrassment to dismissal.

Control and influence

Life sometimes seems out of control and for good reason—you seemingly can control little of what happens around you because the reins often rest in others' hands. Is there a way to wrest them back so that you have a greater degree of say in life's outcomes?

There is a way, which is to focus on influence instead of control, since you influence more things in life than you control. By definition, influence means that you do not direct the outcome, but rather use your position, experience, relationships, status, and other means to affect a decision, project, task, or group of colleagues. The point is that, although you may not be able to control events, you can often influence them to some extent. Through your influence, you have the ability to color their eventual outcome.

An important change in your life occurs when you consciously decide to use your influence and lobby for change. This is a much more active strategy than to stand passively by while events swirl around, and leave you to wonder what would have happened "if" you would have gotten more involved. Seize the moment and leverage your ability to influence. When you know what your limits are, you can focus on a more concentrated set of objectives. This strategy increases your potential. Your aim will be at a defined target rather than a random shot. You will be surprised at how many opportunities you encounter, and how much influence you actually wield once you commit to become more actively involved.

The reason you want to focus on influence rather than control is simple … you have more ability to influence than control. There is nearly always someone more senior than you at work. This person has more control <u>and</u> influence than you possess in your current role. Accept this, but also understand that no matter what your position may be, you have areas of responsibility that you control and others that you can definitely influence. They may not be as broad and general as those of higher ranked individuals, but they exist, nonetheless. Know what your boundaries are and initially focus there. Your knowledge, experience, and skills give you a basis for influence that can be leveraged to both your employer's advantage as well as your own, when done judiciously and intelligently.

To put this into perspective, look at how influence peddling in politics is viewed. It is not a pretty picture and voters are totally fed up with it. Conversely, a physician may request a Zoning Board to permit a variance for the expansion of a clinic she owns that provides needed services to the community. This influences the Board for the common good and for the benefit of the physician. Everyone wins.

This balance between what you can control and what you can influence tends to swing more towards control as you become more experienced and hold positions that are more senior. It is common that you will be required to control more items as a natural consequence of your position and your seniority. Do not attempt to rush this process, but rather govern your actions by the variables that enable you: experience, maturity, knowledge, tenure, skill set, and your level of respect in the organization.

POWERPOINT

INTERNAL MARKETING

The projection of your brand value should be a fundamental part of your internal marketing program. Internal marketing is how you create and sustain the image you want others to associate with you. When you are serious about your career, attention to internally marketing yourself can't be left to chance, but must be given the constant attention it deserves.

Timely completion of work, enlightened meeting participation, internal networking, goal attainment, selective volunteering, project leadership, and active participation in problem solving are just some ways to facilitate your internal marketing plan.

Always work towards who you want to become so that others perceive you in the image that you want to project.

Agent of change

Agents of change are some of the most valuable assets that an organization may employ. These key players don't carry this as an official title, but instead they lead the company from where it is to where it is going. They are the mechanisms by which organizations evolve, grow, and become better tomorrow than they were yesterday. Some people are change agents by their very nature. They are not satisfied with the status quo, and always look for ways to improve the current state. They are the leaders who initiate the bulk of the business transformation work — another name for change—that happens within any organization. Others learn to become agents of change because they train themselves to see better ways to do things and how to get things done. The rest of the working population is happy with the way things are; they accept the status quo and may actually be resistant to change. Which are you? You should know, and if you don't, you should do some self exploration and find out. You can help or hinder. Cause or solve. Change or resist. When it comes to issues that you encounter on the job, you have a choice: promote their continuance through inaction, enable them through ignorance, passively stand by and be a victim, or diligently work to overcome them.

Vibrant organizations welcome change as a necessary component of growth and evolution. Static organizations conversely tend to resist change, remain wedded to old practices, and subsequently lose their place in the market.

The change agent role is not limited to executives. They are found throughout all levels of the organization. You can be a change agent as an entry level hire. When, for example, you are new to your role, you can suggest change provided that you are patient. These suggestions are best accomplished after you get past your initial "settling in" period, wherein you learn the basics of your role and establish yourself as a solid performer. It's not good to walk in the door and immediately begin to recommend how to change the world. This irritates those who have come before you and labels you as a person who is prone to maverick style behavior. Neither ingratiates you to the powers that be. Give yourself enough time to learn your job properly, and in the way it is taught to you. You may not agree one hundred percent with the way it is taught, but learn it anyway.

As you survey the landscape to determine whether you want to become actively involved in a business transformation effort, you should be cognizant of what can you actually change and what it may potentially cost you in personal and professional terms. The foundational question should be, "Is the creation of this transformation worth the benefit that I receive?" What's in it for you? This may sound very self-centered, but it goes far beyond personal loss or gain. The suggestion of alternatives for how things are done in an organization brings a personal cost. The strategy here should be the same as you take with any investment where there is the potential for personal gain or loss. You should receive something in return for what you invest. This can be recognition, satisfaction, or it may be that makes your work easier. Your self-check should be that, similar to any investment, you need to receive something in return for what you invest. This return is often what incents us to want to do even more.

When you decide it is time to suggest changes, ensure you have a logical, programmed approach. You want to be able to document your proposal as well as its value, cost (if any), and risks. As you reach a more mature career point, you will arrive at a place where your suggested changes can impact a broader part of the organization. This requires thought and preparation, and because of the potential for wider impact, should not be addressed without a solid plan. Document your thoughts along with timelines, responsibilities, accountabilities, those with whom you should consult, and those that need to be informed of your proposed actions. Further, socialize ideas for input and possible refinement before going public with your suggested change plan. This permits you to get feedback for improvement before the fact, and build a support base for your suggestion.

All of this takes effort and, when you are the primary agent of change, it may entail that you place your reputation and perhaps your job on the line. This is quite an investment cost. It is also why you must insert yourself into these situations wisely, and ensure there is something in it for you. Ask yourself the tough questions that are relevant to your proposition before you seek a stage for it. Ensure that you investigate risk, mitigations, gains, losses, as well as financial implications.

Determine whether there are political considerations attached to the scope of your transformation proposal, and prepare accordingly. Be thorough, since you are about to step into the spotlight and you want the outcome to be positive.

Change begins with your role and at your immediate level within the organization. It can mean modifications to an operations manual (actual or virtual) that guides your own work. It may also extend beyond your personal world and include impact that is organization-wide. Ensure that you know the scale of the impact that your suggested proposal includes. Do not be afraid to offer a sweeping, broad brush initiative, but make sure that when you do, it is crafted with a plan that is in harmony with its scope. Pick your situations wisely as you are measured by how well you participate, your degree of professionalism, and eventually what the outcome may be.

Become THE expert on one thing

Attention to the growth of your personal value and conscious effort towards enhancement of your brand are both important disciplines that ensure you are well thought of at all levels in the workplace. Your initiative in these areas serves you well when the organization needs to cut back on headcount and also when it looks to fill vacant positions through promotion from within. The best way to maximize your chances for retention in tough times and advancement when times are good is to add incremental personal value.

One method that accomplishes this and draws positive attention to you is to establish yourself as THE expert on at least one key item. What item that may be is totally dependent upon your knowledge base, position, and the role you play. Look around you, and take stock of what would be useful to both yourself and your colleagues. Develop a new skill, learn a process, or hone an existing aspect of your job to a fine edge. Become the "go to" person who is sought out when expertise in your chosen area is required.

One of my sales people took it upon himself to learn the intricacies of how to submit bids for state purchasing contracts. Our company did not participate in that arena, but he was curious and learned the process. When the economy went into a swoon, we looked for ways to increase revenue. This individual became the person to whom we turned for our information. He was subsequently linked with our legal and contracting departments in order to build the service back end. Eventually, he was given the leadership position for state and local government as well as education sales.

The odd point to mention is that some of his sales colleagues thought he was lucky to receive that role. Nothing could be farther from the truth. His desire to learn, his innate inquisitiveness, desire to succeed, and specific knowledge made him the perfect candidate.

He became THE expert to whom we turned when we a problem needed solved. There was no other choice.

POWERPOINT

BE COMMITTED

Success comes to those who are able to commit themselves and not simply be casual in how they attack what is in front of them. When faced with a challenge, a moment of introspection naturally occurs wherein you ask yourself if, and to what degree, you should commit yourself. This relates back to the Old School axiom, "If a job is worth doing, it is worth doing right." In order to do a job well, it takes commitment to properly plan and execute. The degree of commitment invested is reflected in the quality of the outcome.

Commitment to those items in your life that you touch creates drive and passion. This propels you forward and pulls others along with you. Commit to whatever you spend your time doing. You are only given so much time on earth, so use it wisely. Commitment is one way to ensure that you do not squander that gift.

Self-actualization in the work place

As you become more experienced, successful, and your approach to life and work becomes more natural and less forced, you evolve towards the state of self-actualization. For this discussion, I use a rather simplistic definition which states that the process of self-actualization is progress towards realizing your full potential. The important point to note is while you may never fully attain this condition, progress happens provided you are conscientious and apply yourself diligently and thoughtfully.

There will be a point in your career where you excel at certain elements not only on a task level, but on a theoretical plane as well. You will not have to think about how to strategize a path forward, or how to execute it in order to be successful. The correct and logical choice is almost instinctive. The sum of your past experiences and knowledge guides your response with little conscious thought. When you reach this state, you are said to be self-actualized as it relates to this particular element of your being.

You must periodically perform self-checks on your skill and competency levels that affect your work life. These are used as gauges to mark growth and to plot your progress. As you become more senior and experienced, you find that you excel in certain areas wherein you naturally demonstrate competence, skill, and excellence. You need to have an awareness of these areas in order to leverage them to your best advantage. This is another way to accentuate the positive elements of your life in order to evolve into a more self-actualized person.

Knowledge that you are skilled and/or expert in certain areas enables a sense of self-confidence that is based in fact, and not bravado. You do not have to second guess yourself when decisions in these areas present themselves. You know that the thought processes you rely upon in these areas are correct, and that they deliver a solution which is the best for the situation at hand. Some label this a state of unconscious competence. Others call is self-actualization. It can be labeled either way. You know when it happens to you, because you don't have to think about the right thing to do—you just do it.

Don't assume you are there yet, though. An arrogant self-assessment is dangerous as it gives false positives that ultimately lead to harm. You must be realistic in your introspective review. When your assessment is incorrect or premature, you make mistakes that are costly. Since the state of self-actualization typically is attained through seniority, experience, and success, you need to be realistic and not too aggressive in the assignment of this trait to yourself. It is, however, important to know that it is a journey, and that through dedication, learning, and experience you may eventually achieve it in at least some aspect of your business life. There is no formula to alert you exactly as to when. No light bulbs flash, or alarms ring. Self-actualization is attained by degrees and occurs in an almost imperceptible fashion as you gain the necessary qualities for achievement over time.

There are many books written about this topic that provide deep dive, psychological explanations about what self-actualization is and how to progress from one level to another. Your goal should be to obtain the knowledge necessary so that this state may gradually become your reality over time. With that knowledge in hand, you should be prepared to make attainment of self-actualization a personal goal.

READINESS REVIEW

How you conduct yourself on the job says a lot about who you are, your career aspirations, your dedication to your work, and both your current and potential value to your employer. It reaches beyond this, though. Your conduct says a lot about the personal you. Your actions indicate the current state of your work-life balance. That is, how your job affects your personal life and vice versa. Since your work has such a broad and deep influence in your private life, it is imperative that you consistently spend sufficient effort on the interplay between these two areas.

You experience measureable improvement on specific items when you discover your personal methodology that enables you to concentrate on them. You also find that the learnings gained from one item empower you to improve the other more effectively. It is a process that builds upon itself. The end product is that the execution of these items becomes increasingly automatic when you consciously focus on their quality execution. It takes time and repetition for certain learnings to take hold and become part of your life. This is why you should pick one item, work on it, make it your own, and then move on to another. The execution of a programmatic strategy over time results in changes that are real and substantial. Measure your progress over sufficient periods of time, build upon each success, and enjoy the results!

A group of co-workers at one of my earlier employers started a book club early one year. We decided we would all buy and read one business book a month. We then met to discuss the current book in progress every two weeks. A year later, each of us had a broad, foundational library of books that we not only read cover-to-cover, but also discussed with our peers. To this day, this is a topic of conversation when I re-connect with those past colleagues. The value this had on our personal development was considerable, and we all acknowledge that we still benefit from that group effort to this day.

Those among us who are not career oriented tend to act without substantial forethought in most work-re-

lated situations. They demonstrate a lack of a defined career plan and simply don't care to have one. While it is not necessary to plot and scheme our every move on and off the job, it is absolutely requisite to be conscious of what you do, how you do it, and with whom you do it with. How you act on the job today goes a long way toward the payment of a handsome dividend at some point in the future. Victory at nearly every endeavor usually goes to those who are prepared. It is extremely difficult to be prepared when you act randomly.

PERSONAL DEVELOPMENT ACTIONS

- List the number of business books you own and how many others (owned or borrowed) that you read in the past three months. When you are passionate about your job, you continually educate yourself. Reading books is one way to accomplish this. What are three others?

- Determine your personal status quo with respect to your work environment. Are you content with how things are today and have no desire for change? Would you prefer some key changes be made and perhaps you would help others make them real? Do you have a burning desire to change the landscape and are ready to commence immediately? If your answer is closer to the latter instead of the former, then you are either an agent of change or a potential agent. List three ways through which you may become involved in the change process in order to fulfill this desire.

- Relate to how much time you typically spend completing a task in order to get it "just right" or perfect. Does the time you spend to get it done to perfection warrant the time invested in those last few percentage points? Does spending thirty per cent more time warrant the gain of five per cent in quality? Is perfection the proper choice in everything you do? Some projects and tasks require perfection while others are best served by rapid completion at a sufficient level of quality.

- Review your knowledge about specific products, processes, and methodologies that are used on the job. Are you the recognized expert for any one of these? Do people come to you for advice or insight related to them? How can you increase your knowledge and let it be known that you are the best available resource for at least one of these? How would this help you without it being seen as a cry for attention?

- Remember that last time something underperformed in your estimation. Were you grossly upset that it did not meet the expectations you set for it? Would you have preferred that the outcome would have been better? How were you affected? Would it have been better without the emotional investment of expectation setting? Review your preparation for an upcoming event. Determine the mental investment that expectation requires versus preference. Which works best for you? Which would permit you to better handle a negative outcome?

CHAPTER THREE
THE BEST OFFENSE STARTS WITH A GOOD DEFENSE

Employment is comparable to an athletic event in many ways. Similar to achievement in sports, success in business depends upon the execution of both offense and defense. Those who have the best defensive capabilities help their offense through the prevention of hostile acts that can hinder them from reaching their goals. This similarity that your job shares with sports suggests that you should hone your defensive skills when you are to go on the offensive and charge ahead. Your good defense minimizes distractions and obstacles. This puts you far ahead of those who do not have both offensive and defensive prowess.

The previous chapter offered various suggestions for improvement that prepares you for opportunities when they present themselves. This, in other words, was a review of how to get organized and get your "offensive" game plan together. This chapter focuses how you can protect yourself—that is, ensure your "defense" is prepared and ready to guard your interests.

Read ahead with the thought in mind of how to improve your capability to protect yourself against negative events and outcomes. Advanced preparation that prevents trouble is more valuable than damage control in the wake of a setback. Similar to martial arts training, the guidance is to avoid conflict. When you encounter situations where conflict is unavoidable, however, be prepared to engage and win. Loss is not an option. The preferred mindset is again proactive versus reactive.

Your internal reputation

How others perceive you may not be how you believe they do. Self-perception is a flawed measurement device. It offers only a limited perspective and one that is often tainted by your own prejudice, ego and, possibly, delusions. It is a one hundred eighty degree look at a subject that is very important to you—and that is yourself. While one hundred eighty degrees may seem to be a rather complete assessment, what is actually needed is a full circle, 360° review that includes others' perceptions as well as your own.

When your personal 360° review is done in the workplace, it should include those above you, your peers, and your subordinates, if this category applies. Some organizations employ a software tool to accomplish 360° reviews. It is often done as an improvement exercise on a periodic basis through the Human Resources department. When your company participates in this type of activity, you have the tool to use at your disposal. On the other hand, if you do not have access to the tool or do not trust the results it produces, then you have to manually complete this exercise yourself. You must carry out the task honestly and objectively, if it is to benefit you.

The data collection exercise can take many forms. You may want to wait until your interim or annual review to begin. This is an appropriate time since this is when your manager shares their perceptions with you. This gives you the first component, and, therefore, is a great place to begin. You may then take the next step and begin to gather peer input. This may be awkward, but provided that it is done in a manner that encourages honest input without discomfort, it can be done. The key point here is to be sensitive as to how you approach others. You may wish to begin with those with whom you work, as well as how you believe they perceive you. Do not include everyone, but make your list a representative sample of those with whom you have both direct and indirect contact. The key here is to be casual and informal. Formality puts them on the defensive. This can be done over coffee in the break room or other neutral territory. You may begin with a simple ice breaker question such as "I wonder how people think we are doing at our jobs?" This positions your conversation as a discussion about your team or work group, and not directly about you. You can then get feedback of a more personal nature within the context of that conversation. "Do you believe I am thought of as a key contributor?" would narrow the focus to you. It asks for an opinion, so be ready for anything. This is not the time to be weak hearted or argumentative. When you don't want an honest answer, don't ask the question.

If you are a manager, you may then move your discussion to your direct reports. Since you are in a position of authority, you could simply poll your team about how they perceive working conditions, which include their view of how you manage. This can be done in a team setting or during one-on-one meetings. It is always good to periodically ask your team how you are doing anyway, as it provides them a chance for them to offer feedback.

Be selective in the choice of whom you speak with In the course of this exercise and filter the input of those who do and do not matter. While this may seem to be a judgmental and arrogant methodology, it is actually necessary if you are to complete an accurate assessment. Some colleagues may be so erroneously prejudiced either for or against you that their opinion must be discredited.

Your primary goal of this exercise is to gain an understanding of your internal reputation. While either methodology is not one hundred per cent accurate, each does provide a glimpse into how you are thought of by a variety of people in different roles. Use this information wisely and to your advantage. Accentuate the positives and minimize the negatives.

POWERPOINT

REPUTATIONS ARE AS FRAGILE AS GLASS

Most of us work in a public place. This is especially true in today's cubicle office environment and even extends to those who work from a home office. Modern communications create a sense of presence that exposes you to all eyes and ears. When you're at work, you are on stage—it is live theater. You need to act as if everyone is looking at you, because they are.

The positive things you do in the performance of your job are expected. That is why you were hired in the first place. What stand out are your notable achievements and any public disasters. The sad fact is that the glow of achievement has a short half life, while, conversely, the lingering effects of negative events go on forever. Years of hard work and positive contribution can become irrelevant due to one misdeed or error of judgment.

This goes beyond work and includes your public life as well. An executive with whom I worked was arrested for driving under the influence. This ruined his career. Other examples abound, but the end result of all of them is that jobs are lost and careers ruined by things that happen in an instant.

Consider the broader consequences of your actions, because once enacted, it is impossible to retract them.

Conflict

Conflict in the workplace is inevitable. Eventually, it either finds you, or you find it. You go to work one day and discover yourself in some type of disagreement with another person or persons. You could also find yourself at odds with a business practice that is non-productive, or another situation that you simply can't let pass unaddressed. Expect it and you won't be surprised when it happens, because it will. It's at this time that you are faced with decisions that have the potential to change your entire life. Therefore, it is necessary that you determine beforehand what your tolerance level is for conflict when measured against your values, morals, ethics, and professional standards. Also, reflect on your willingness to engage at the time you are confronted with the situation, and decide what level of engagement the conflict demands. These issues often have the potential for escalation, and consequences may be severe. Balance the risk versus reward and plan your actions accordingly. Understand that not every situation demands a reaction, and not all reactions need to be addressed at full throttle.

When you're faced with a potentially inflammatory situation, quickly decide if you should or should not engage. Battles in the workplace are usually polarizing, and seldom result in win-win situations for those involved. Instead, there is most likely a winner and a loser. Furthermore, the person who is right is not always the winner. What this means is that you need to determine how to pick your battles, and which to avoid all together.

Does this necessarily mean that you plan in advance for upcoming conflict? No, but it does mean to have a sense of awareness that trouble is brewing. Does it mean that you wait until trouble happens, quickly weigh your options, and make spontaneous decisions? My guidance here is neither. Instead of these, there is another, more productive strategy that should be considered. Know yourself and what pushes or pulls you to become involved in disputes. Know your triggers and your hot buttons. Be confident in yourself, your skills, and your values. Know what your tolerance levels are for challenges to these. Finally, do the right thing on a consistent basis and lessen the chance for differences to occur. It is always best to stop the storm before it strikes. This way, the conflict does not have to lead to a confrontation, since it does not happen.

Before any action is taken, determine what the most positive and negative outcomes could be, and only then decide if either is worth the trouble of engagement. Some fights are simply not worth fighting, while others are. This is a decision that you must make as each situation is different. When you challenge a broken process that improves the organization, the outcome should not damage you, even if it is less than ideal. When, on the other hand, you are the victim of intimidation or harassment, the potential for disruption of your life as well as that of others is considerable. The personal effects of the pursuit of these types of cases can be intense. You may be traumatized to a great degree as you fight for what is right. In some of these instances, you will find the battle is worth the fight, and in other cases it may be better to move on or, in drastic cases, even leave your current employer. This is a very personal decision that may have far reaching consequences. This potential must be weighed carefully prior to taking action.

Anytime there is a dispute on the job, it should be handled in a manner which minimizes the amount of emotion and maximizes the use of logic. Emotion colors the story and does not permit an accurate evaluation of the situation. Furthermore, parties in a conflict who display emotion are typically less likely to be believed than those who present their story calmly and with facts in hand. While this is not always the case, it is a guideline that should unfailingly be used whether you are alone, or where a third party (manager, Human Resources, or other) is brought into play.

Perhaps the worst instance of conflict occurs when there is a violation of your personal rights (I.E. discrimination or harassment). In this case, it is an absolute necessity to notify proper authorities about the breach. When your rights are violated, you are bound to act to not only protect yourself, but to offer protection to others that may be similarly affected. This can't, however, be done vicariously, or without considerable thought beforehand. These are serious issues, and there needs to be documentation, witnesses, and/or other corroborating evidence that wrongdoing is either ongoing or has occurred in the recent past. It is vital that this type of accusation not be discussed with work friends, other employees, or as water cooler talk because this could backfire and cause the accusation to be turned against you. You must prepare your case well with your background complete before you go to proper authorities. "Proper authorities" can be Human Resources, legal, compliance, government agencies, and, in extreme cases, law enforcement.

Other conflicts that may occur are of a less serious nature, but they must be faced in a similar manner. For this reason, you have to know the difference between personal conflict and general business differences. Disagreements can happen at personal, departmental, and company-wide levels and can also include disagreements between certain individuals or groups of individuals.

You will also encounter what may be called normal life conflicts along the way as well. These are not earthshaking, nor do they require trips to Human Resources or an attorney. In the end, though, they do need to be handled in much the same way as other the differences covered above. Take a measured approach with time spent in consideration of the possible consequences of your potential engagement. Your reaction to these circumstances should be to follow classic conflict resolution steps: recognize that differences exist, listen non-judgmentally, don't place blame but let the other person know how their actions made you feel, and finally, learn from the interaction then move on. Many times you may actually earn a new ally or supporter if you logically address an issue and apply a win-win perspective to the issue at hand.

POWERPOINT

CONTROL YOUR EMOTIONS

Co-workers, your boss, those you manage, and those whom you encounter on the job prefer to work with colleagues who are even tempered and level headed. Some people are alienated by those who become too excited about success or too down about failure. Honest introspection helps you determine how moody you are in the work place. You may need to self-govern your mood swings to keep them within a range that leads to the perception that you are neither a hot head nor a loose cannon. You want to be thought of as a level-headed thinker who reacts well in all situations. Your attitude affects others as well as yourself, and is a key point related to how you are perceived by others.

A manager at a mortgage company would come to work with his personal life displayed on his face. When his family life was going well, he was happy and jovial. If not, the opposite would be the norm. His team would gauge his mood before they engaged him to determine (as they came to say), "... if he took the red pill or the blue pill today." On days when his mood was dark and the team achieved their goals, he would not celebrate their success. On the contrary, on days when performance was sub-par but his mood was upbeat, he would be overtly positive. This created confusion in the team. They looked to their manager for leadership, but what they got in return was confusing, inconsistent feedback.

Scapegoats

In business, when a problem arises, someone must be held accountable. Sadly, too much energy is spent on this, and not enough on prevention or resolution. Blame for issues or negative outcomes is all too often assigned to an easy target—a scapegoat—and not to the true person or persons responsible for the problem.

Be aware of the fact that this is a common practice in business. When a project begins to sour, those individuals who believe they are the most threatened frequently begin to survey the landscape for a scapegoat. They seek out someone to whom blame may be attached, so they are shielded against possible negative consequences. In order to protect yourself against these actions, it is imperative to ensure that your contribution is well documented and associated work is performed in a quality manner. Escalate issues quickly to the proper person and document this interaction. Do not believe for a minute that verbal agreements regarding your positive contribution suffice when it comes to the attachment of a name to a failure. Always expect the worst, and be pleasantly surprised if the opposite occurs. The written word and associated documentation is what counts.

Look for the signs of the blame game early in its genesis. These signs can be statements made in person, comments on a call, or within an email. You may see certain groups begin to "circle their wagons" for self-preservation (this is often done when a group makes misleading proclamations about the work in progress to those in authority). Other times there are outright statements that call into question someone's contribution or work quality. The signs are usually transparent to someone who has their eyes open and who pays attention.

It is important to ensure you are not the next target on the horizon. You must always be aware and measure your "target-ability." By this, I mean your potential exposure to become a scapegoat when danger signs lurk on the horizon. Pay attention to your environment. Are key meetings that you previously attended now held without you? If so, you must make it a priority to find out why. Have you contributed as agreed or assigned? Have your accomplishments been properly recognized and documented? If not, then you must take steps to overcome this deficiency before it is too late, and you become a target. Have you raised risks and possible mitigations associated with your work in a documented manner and to the correct person or group? If not, then remedy ASAP (and don't let it happen again!).

Your next step is to determine if you are in a position to succeed or a position to fail. When you find yourself about to be placed in a "no win" situation, you should not accept the role, as it has built-in failure attached. Point out why you will not accept it in a respectful manner, but do not assume the work. When forced to accept it by a superior, document your concerns respectfully in an email, and let them know in bullet points what your issues are and how/if you believe they can be mitigated. Do not rely upon the spoken word or oral agreement—they are meaningless.

Stay out of the soup

Empire building, self-aggrandizement, covert agendas, overt agendas, and similar behaviors are common in business. They are examples of the sources which drive organizational turf battles. These are internal struggles wherein the combatants jostle for control of various departments or other prizes within the organization in order to establish or extend power. They regularly recruit support for their cause and sooner or later, they will attempt to recruit you. They try to get you "in the soup." This is similar to the game we played as kids, where someone was caught in the middle of the group that played keep-away with a ball. When caught in the adult version, you find few options through which you can extricate yourself. Your best choice is simply to stay out of the soup and remain neutral. There is so much to lose and very little to gain.

Seldom do these games provide positive benefits to all involved, and rarely are they a plus to those who become intertwined with them. They usually benefit the winning players and more specifically, only those high enough in the food chain to reap the rewards of victory. Everyone else becomes a bystander who feels the side effects of the outcome, and little more. They might receive a nod of thanks, but in the vast majority of cases their reward is not in balance with their support. Those who supported the loser carry that stigma until they move on or have the good fortune to pick a winner ... next time.

It is simply a statement of fact that certain people or groups always try to further their causes, and that their associated activities often have deleterious effects on those caught in the middle. It is acceptable to remain neutral, and let the powers-to-be conduct their power struggle. One thing is for certain: you do not want to place yourself in the middle of a corporate turf war that you have no ability to influence. Further, it is not a bright idea to be involved in turf battles in which you stand to gain little and possibly lose everything. Workers tend to polarize around work issues. They gossip, project their thoughts, make predictions, and solicit input from others. When you observe this behavior, it is best to ignore it and get on with what you were hired to do—be a productive employee. Serious repercussions may occur when you place yourself on one side or the other of an issue. That which you stand to gain is usually not worth your potential exposure to loss. Be cognizant of your risk to reward ratio.

Be aware of manipulation

The manipulation of others in order to achieve personal goals is a common characteristic often seen on the job. Although not everyone exhibits this trait, be constantly aware of its presence. Co-workers or managers may manipulate others for their own purposes, so remain alert as this can come at you from any direction. A measured amount of paranoia applied to others' actions can go a very long way to inoculate you against its effects. One of the worst feelings is to realize too late that you have been manipulated by someone. It makes you feel used, abused, and devalued.

Some people manipulate consciously while others do it unconsciously. The conscious manipulators are perhaps the easiest to identify as they tend to be somewhat transparent in their actions and objectives. They have an agenda that is easy to spot, and they do little to hide it. These are typically one-sided, self-serving individuals who manipulate others to obtain what they can't achieve through their own merits.

An excellent example was the manager of a group of process designers who had her sights set on selection into her company's executive training program. She assigned her team to support only members of management who were on the selection committee. This created a dearth of support bandwidth for anyone else. This became blatantly clear in a very short time and her ruse was identified, which caused her plan to backfire. Her clear manipulation of her subordinates for her personal gain was obvious and blatantly unethical.

Unconscious manipulators are often more difficult to spot, and therefore avoid. These people have a built-in defect that is a natural part of how they conduct themselves. This tends to hide their manipulative ways, since it is an organic behavior. Once spotted and identified, be wary of their intentions, and always be on the alert so as to ensure that you are not drawn unwittingly into a less than productive scenario. Managers, for instance, who place unrealistic due dates on their teams to look good to their superiors often do this without even a thought about the consequences. It becomes an unconscious act of team manipulation that, unless identified by the team or the manager's superiors, continues to the detriment of all.

Manipulation should not be confused with honest efforts to cobble together support for initiatives or programs that are for the benefit of the organization. Colleagues who champion these are polar opposites from those who manipulate. They work with the organization's best interests in mind and do not attempt to advance their own agendas. Learn to recognize the difference and act accordingly when confronted by each. This is a skill that is gained through observation and, regretfully, through experience.

If you suspect you are a victim, you have a couple choices, neither of which is glamorous or guaranteed to make you feel better. The first is to honor your commitment and learn from your naiveté. The second is to confront the manipulator in a controlled fashion and state that you no longer wish to participate. Both of these choices are productive only if you take your medicine and learn. There is no better way to become aware about manipulation than to be on the receiving end of someone's display of this behavior.

POWER POINT

PICK UP A PHONE

Effective communication—that is, the clear exchange of information with proper contacts within acceptable time frames—is a key to understanding your position and intentions as well as those of others. Email can be misleading and certain nuances can't be interpreted with any degree of accuracy. Do not fall into the trap of top heavy reliance on email to communicate. Use email only once per topic when you deal with a colleague. If you do not receive an answer in an appropriate time, pick up the phone and call them. Do not avoid calling your co-worker, since it permits direct contact and facilitates

---

a more robust discussion of the topic at hand. When your phone call does not result in contact, leave a voice mail that includes when and why you called. Include a time when you will call back. Your next alternative is to see the individual in person. This should be done with sensitivity to the protocol required for this meeting. When a topic is important enough to discuss, then a programmed escalation of communication methods is justifiable.

In ??? we trust

There are times when you may be asked to offer your support or allegiance with a particular person. This support may be in the form of your vote on a topic under consideration, backing for a project, help with an initiative, or similar activity. You should immediately become wary when someone asks you to personally support them. If you choose to provide your support, it should only be for a reason that is important to you and not just them. While this should never be a common practice, ensure that it is for a good reason and with the correct individual.

Very few people actually deserve your trust or allegiance. The few who do stand out from the crowd and consistently display characteristics that indicate they are not self-serving. Rather, their actions demonstrate they are pro-company, pro-employee, pro-customer, and most importantly, pro-you. It is extremely difficult to fake these characteristics because they make dishonorable people nervous and uncomfortable. Their true self shows through beneath their transparent veneer. It cannot be hidden for extended periods of time.

When you decide to offer support, make sure you know what you are getting into. Why do they need your backing? What is the issue at hand? Who is the person? What is the up and down side of your potential involvement? When you are satisfied with what you discover and the answers to your queries are positive, then you may make your move. If, however, there is any element of doubt, remain neutral until a time when you are convinced that the offer of your support is the correct thing to do. You are not bound to prop up any individual at work. You may agree to provide help, encouragement, assistance, or a host of other synonyms, but be very careful about outright political backing for any individual on the job. This should be extended in only the most select situations where you have much more to gain than to lose, and where the character of the individual is impeccable.

Don't always say "Yes"

This is a delicate subject. It is relevant to people who are extremely productive, but who work in an environment that may be unappreciative. These individuals may fear reprisals if they refuse to take on additional tasks, no matter what the circumstances. Another reason is that they may want to please management, and feel they need to accept everything that comes their way. This frequently includes deadlines for delivery or the expanding scope of a project. These may have little or no basis in reality, or need, but they are piled onto the employee nonetheless.

When you are always available and say "Yes" to every task or job thrown at you, you run the risk of being taken for granted. Further, even though you may produce top quality work, the volume of your output becomes the focus, and not its quality. When you are always at the ready, as a loyal Labrador dog that pants and eagerly waits for its master to say "Yes," then your owner (manager) will simply throw the ball, and you run to fetch it.

It takes a conscious effort to not only produce top quality work, but to complete it in the appropriate volumes that satisfy the needs of the company. Your production must generate the respect that should be yours as a consequence of your efforts and skills. Many deadlines for deliverables in the workplace are artificial. They are attached to promises that have been made without proper consultation with the teams that do the work, and, consequently, make the promises good. This can lead to the teams becoming unwitting victims, which is an uncomfortable position nobody wants to be in.

When you can tactfully constrain access to what you produce without being seen as a "slacker," your work output is appreciated more. The delicate art of saying "No" assists in the maintenance of your sanity and, in the long run, the quality of your work.

Too much productivity can hurt

Management is often not bright or insightful enough to recognize that some people produce high volumes of quality work on a routine basis. They tend to manage toward the norm, and associate work done quickly with work done poorly. Routine completion of high quality output ahead of schedule can lead to negative consequences if your manager is someone who does not manage with their eyes open. It is fine to beat your deadline more often than not, but beware if it becomes the norm, especially when you are managed by someone who does not appreciate the difference between superior and average performance.

When you are a high performance contributor who completes tasks ahead of time in a quality fashion, you open the door for being taken advantage of by less than fully evolved leaders. These types may throw tasks at you because they know that you will do what is necessary to get them done with little or no thought to the personal impact of the work on your private life. They know that if the task is not completed during work hours, your weekend will be spent on your deliverable while they enjoy guilt free time off. These same managers frequently take your superior output for granted and not give you the credit that you rightly earn through your efforts. The fact that they do not recognize your high performance, and do not appreciate your exceptional levels of quality, should set off alarms. This is a great example of the necessity to work with your *Eyes Wide Open*™ so that you are not taken advantage of, and actually receive the rewards that are consistent with your contribution. The guidance here is to excel, but do so in a measured manner that is in line with your situation.

Great products (and you are a product within the eyes of your management) are never easily obtained and usually come at a premium. Gold and diamonds are valuable because they are rare. When you are too ready to work weekends or late nights on a routine basis and sacrifice your personal life for work, your constant availability devalues your work.

Your contribution may also be minimized by some managers who could perceive you as a talented individual who is easily manipulated for their own personal gain. I have seen managers of high performing subordinates accept rewards that should have been shared or passed through to their rightful owner. These subordinates' quality work was much too easily available, since they were over eager to please. They felt that their manager would "take care of them" and ensure that they would be recognized for their efforts. This mistake ultimately is seen as a weakness, and not a strength. It will subsequently be used to manipulate you again and again, when it is one of your characteristics. Remember that it's fine to occasionally work extra hours to get rush projects completed, but never make it a routine way to execute tasks related to your position.

Sleep on major or emotional decisions

Major decisions should not be rushed into, but instead need careful consideration before action is taken. Seldom do these potentially life-changing events need to be handled immediately. They typically offer some time for reflection and thought. It is wise to take advantage of this time, and mull over the ramifications of the decision you are about to make. Time spent in deliberation about the possible outcomes and their effect on you is time that you can ill afford not to spend. Further, do not permit yourself to be forced into an emotional decision by someone who needs an answer "now." This is the old hard sell, used car sales trick, and the person who asks you to make such a decision is disrespectful of you. Be mindful of this ruse, and do not let that individual bully you into a hasty decision. In fact, when faced with this situation, be even more alert to possible secondary motives that may not be in your best interests.

It is always best to sleep on major or emotional decisions before you make them. When you do not react immediately, but rather allow some time to pass before you offer your response, chances of a more carefully thought out and considered response go up dramatically. Time tends to put things into perspective and gives you the opportunity to examine an issue from all points of view. Time also provides your subconscious the opportunity to work on the item under consideration during your down time or sleep. New insights into the situation which enable you to respond in a more objective manner happen when you use this tactic. It is not uncommon to go to sleep with a problem on your mind only to awake the next morning with the solution before you.

Your employer has NO loyalty to you

You owe your employer a good day's work for a good day's pay. That is the contract—either real or implied. If you believe the company owes you anything more, then you are naïve, and on the dimly lit road to disappointment. When you deliver superior performance, you enhance your chances of being recognized for a job well done, and at the same time, enhance the opportunity to increase your pay and possibly other benefits. This should be how you prefer to be treated. You are simply out of touch with reality if you expect it. If you believe your employer always has your best interests in mind and is loyal to you, get over it. You are a fool with your head in the clouds when you think they do. Their first duty is to the health of the organization. Everything else is secondary and plays a supporting role. It is incredible how many people think their employer will take care of them beyond their paycheck and benefits.

Employers constantly calculate the cost to recruit, hire, train, and retain their employees. These line items on the budget spreadsheet are included the operating expense (OpEx) of an organization. Companies have operating expense targets that they aim to achieve during each fiscal measurement period (I.E. quarter, fiscal year). The cost of labor is a substantial portion of any company's OpEx. When the operating expenses exceed target, the company often looks to a reduction in labor cost to ensure they meet their OpEx objective for the next measurement period. This means layoffs, reductions in force, or right-sizing. Whatever the label, it means lost jobs.

Do you believe your employer will not lay you off because you have bills and that you've done your job satisfactorily? Will they retain the average worker over the superior producer because the average employee has been there longer? I would not bet on either of the above. You do, however, increase your chances for retention when you build a reputation for excellence, apply what you learn in this book, and establish a record of productivity that makes you the clear choice to retain. There are no guarantees, though, since there is no loyalty.

Lying ... career death

Once caught in a lie, you might as well find another job with another company as your career with your current employer is most assuredly over. The act of lying is a sign of bad character. It is said that when a person tells a lie on one occasion, they have told lies before, and will lie again. This needs no explanation—it is a simple rule.

Your integrity must be protected at all costs. This means being one hundred per cent truthful. Never stretch the truth or tell any form of lie. Stand up for the truth even if you believe that your honesty could have a negative impact on you. Any impact is only in the short term, if there is any less than desirable effect at all. In fact, you will probably be seen as someone who is mature enough to accept responsibility, and admired for that strength. The fact is that a lie once told reflects even more negatively than any truth you attempt to cover up, and the effects of your dishonesty are permanent. Nothing you can do changes the words once they leave your lips.

This extends to the acceptance of responsibility for those things that go wrong for which you are truly to blame. Everyone makes mistakes. This includes you. When something happens for which you are at fault, accept the responsibility and do not attempt to deflect it for some weak reason or to another individual. It is what it is, and you need to accept the fact that you are to blame. You also need to step up and suggest how to remedy or mitigate the damage. This puts a corrective action plan in place to ensure that the same thing will not happen again.

READINESS REVIEW

Self-defense is always a good skill to have at your disposal. While martial arts can protect you in physical altercations, you need a less physical, more cerebral skill set at work to ensure you properly defend yourself. However, you need to be vigorous in your preparations for work-related self-protection, much as you would as when you practice a martial arts skill. This may be accomplished by multiple methods, but, as in martial arts training, there is one tactic that should be learned and applied in an intelligent manner ... learn to avoid trouble.

The proactive avoidance of conflict and trouble prevent you from the need to expend energy and time on conflict resolution. It takes you out of combat situations, and permits you to remain productive. Avoidance also often confuses your potential adversary, since they typically assume (making assumptions is their problem, not yours) that you will engage and that a battle will ensue. Surprise is always an ally, so learn to use it as such.

If, however, engagement is inevitable, learn how to protect yourself and how to do so effectively. To paraphrase what Indiana Jones said to his adversary in Raiders of the Lost Ark, "You shouldn't bring a knife to a gun fight." Preparation is one key to success in this area. This chapter provides a robust baseline of required skills. It should not matter if the attack comes from above, below, or from a peer level. Preparation allows you to avoid trouble. When pressed, vigorously defend yourself so that you are the last man standing when the dust settles.

PERSONAL DEVELOPMENT ACTIONS

- Remember the last time you saw someone at work "lose it" emotionally. How did that make you feel? How did others react to the outburst? Was it productive or could another route have been taken that would have had a more positive feeling? List what your top tools are for keeping control of your emotions.

- Review the last time you were involved in an email thread that extended to three or more replies. Could the issue have been more easily and accurately addressed if you would have picked up the phone and dialed the other party? Direct contact works best. An entry in your daily log would document the discussion. Resolve not become involved in long email threads in the future. Instead, call someone directly after no more than two exchanges.

- Make a list of what you believe three people at work would say about you if asked. Would the comments of your manager be different from those of co-workers? What would these comments say about your internal reputation? It is critical to monitor your reputation closely and not to act randomly. This places the maintenance of your reputation in the forefront of your mind and permits you to monitor and nurture it consistently.

- Think back to a situation when you went to bed with an unsolved problem on your mind. You woke up the next morning with a fresh point of view and the issue solved. Do you tend to react immediately to problems or situations, or do you allow your subconscious mind to moderate your emotions and work through problems? When next faced with a major decision, emotionally charged situation, or problem, do not immediately react but sleep on it before you make your next move.

- Determine what you expect from your employer beyond a paycheck, agreed to benefits, and a safe place to work. Do you believe they owe you anything more? If so, what is it that you believe they owe you? Is this expectation reasonable? At what point do your expectations become unreasonable. Remember, having expectations and not preferences set you up for disappointment. Neither you nor your employer should expect more of the other beyond what is legal and contractually agreed to.

CHAPTER FOUR
PEOPLE: THE CAUSE OR THE CURE?

The saying goes that the world would be a great place if it were not for the people who inhabit it. While this is a rather extreme statement, it does provide some insight into the primary cause of the majority of issues that confront you on the job. That is, the people.

It takes a lifetime of conscious effort to learn how to effectively deal with those with whom you work, and still you will be surprised by something new more often than you might prefer. Most work places are caste systems with a hierarchy of management and their subordinates. You see your co-workers jostle for position, compete for attention, pursue their desire for power—the list could go on for pages. Suffice it to say that you will encounter potentially every type of behavior that can be found in the psychology books while on the job.

You must go to work with your *Eyes Wide Open*™ and your defenses activated. Any other decision can prove harmful to your career as well as your psyche. While I do not advocate that you become totally defense minded and paranoid, I do advise that you prepare yourself through education about what you might find in the road ahead. The ability to recognize both good and bad behaviors will assist you to build an enjoyable and fruitful work experience. You would not walk into a totally dark, unfamiliar room without the lights turned on, but if you ignore this advice and plunge ahead unprepared, you will do exactly that.

In previous chapters, focus was primarily on your state of mind and how to prepare yourself for what lies ahead. It's now time to shift gears and look more closely at the people around you. You may work with them, for them, or even manage them, but no matter how you interact with them, they do influence you. You need to be aware of what that influence means in a multitude of situations.

The mirror of society

A question was once asked about what different types of people are encountered in the workplace. The answer was very pragmatic, "Both good and bad people have to pay bills and feed themselves." Translated, this means that everyone, no matter who they are or what their role is in life, has to make a living in order to meet their obligations and function at some level in our society. You may either be a saint or a sinner, but you still have to eat, clothe yourself, and have some type of roof over your head. That means that, unless you're a career criminal, trust fund baby, or a lottery winner, you have to have a job and earn an income. This is why the workplace is nothing more than a mirror of society. If you ever wanted an example that captures the meaning of the phrase, "It takes all kinds ..." look no further.

As a member of the working community, you interact with this cross section on a daily basis. Your relationships with them influence your ability to do your work and also impact your job satisfaction. For this reason, you need to have an awareness of those with whom you interact while at work. It is crucial to see your co-workers as real people and not just warm bodies with job titles. They impact you on both the human and work levels, so you need to incorporate this into these relationships. Determine who is either a help or a hindrance to your productivity.

This requires that you make some value judgments along the way. These are best made with minimal external influence and kept private after the fact. Little, if any, benefit is provided when you share personal thoughts about others to a third party. This places you in a position to lose plenty and gain nothing. In this context, the advice is to "Keep your eyes wide open and your mouth closed shut."

Quality leadership

Leaders in management and executive positions are similar to all other people throughout an organization that populate its many roles. They theoretically need the knowledge, skills, and experience (often known as the KSEs) that are necessary to perform their job at a high level. They should be sufficiently intelligent and possess the ability to think critically. The ability to know the differences between strategy and tactics, and how to make them both succeed is also key. These individuals should be the best of the best within the organization, since they are responsible not only for the health of the company, but for the mortgages, car payments, college savings plans, and other expenses of everyone within the organization.

A good place to begin your investigation as to who sits in the offices of power is to take note of their backgrounds. A large amount of data can usually be found on LinkedIn, Plaxo, and other professional and social networking sites. A good second source is company biographies on the web or in your annual report. Try a simple Google search as well. It can uncover quite a bit of information that is useful. Many senior execs have multiple Google hits, since they are quoted in industry pub-lications and are more in the public eye than the average employee. View them as if you were hiring them to do the job they now hold. Are they seemingly qualified, or are they in a new situation that leverages certain qualities in the hope they learn how to successfully execute in this role? Are they a fit for the position or not? Allow yourself the lux-ury of a value judgment. It is a good baseline.

Next, find out how they got their job in your organization. If pro-moted from within, did they either obtain their job through a com-petitive process, or did they inherit it through a promotion because of their connections? If they came in from the outside (as an external candidate), were they recruited because they knew someone from a past association, or were they part of a larger pool of candidates who went through a vigorous screening process? This becomes important as it affects not only their fit for the job, but it also has an impact on your organization's culture. Companies that vet their candidates for key roles, whether internal or external, at least do due diligence in their attempt to match the best candidate with the position. Those who simply anoint friends or associates without the performance of due process do the organization a disservice, as more qualified individuals who could have been hired may not have even been interviewed.

Remember the Peter Principle? It is a theory related to incompetence in management. In short, it states that members of an organization are eventually promoted to a level at which they are no longer competent to do their job. A side effect of this is that these same people then find themselves assigned to a role that is beneath their pay grade, because that is in line with their level of competence. Are they over their heads and destined to fail? Let's examine this a bit further.

Do the best salespeople make the best managers? Typically not, since both require much different skill sets and people skills. Those who are promoted through convenience, connections, length of service, and other non-competitive methods are usually not the best candidates. More often than not, they damage the organization and the area of which they are in command, because their core skills in sales do not transfer to the skills needed to effectively manage people. Of course, there are exceptions, but businesses are not successfully run by exceptions. Instead, the highest performing organizations are run by general rule.

Great leaders have to have a track record of successful leadership that is developed over time. Greatness does not happen overnight. Their leadership skills must be an element of their core competency. They do not wake up one day and discover they are leaders of men. Of course, some top leaders possess a variety of the innate, essential attributes necessary to be leaders, but even these must be continuously improved upon in order for them to remain effective.

Many of our best leaders do not have a job-related specialty in which they excel, but perform at a high level across multiple functions. They may also have a superior grasp of their business as a whole, which provides a generalist's perspective of the organization. This is an asset for strategic development, since it provides a cross functional view of the business. A Chief Information Officer (CIO), for example, may create an excellent technical infrastructure for their company. He may not, however, have the vision and leadership qualities that compel people to follow him. He should not, therefore, be promoted to CEO just because he has been there the longest and is known by the Board of Directors. There are probably better choices available. I saw an example of this at a well known Fortune 500 company, and the results were catastrophic. One of the good old boys with questionable KSE's was elevated to CEO without the benefit of a competitive process. The company's general population quickly lost their passion, clients departed, and financial results suffered across the board.

Also pay close attention to whom your leaders import for support after they are hired. Do they look outside of the company at old colleagues to fill key roles that support them, or do they take the time to get to know qualified internal candidates? All too often, outsiders bring in more outsiders and stifle the career paths of existing staff. This absolutely kills the incentive to perform and damages the organization's culture for the sake of convenience and comfort. This is an easy item for you to get the answer to, and one that should be closely monitored as new blood comes into the organization. It says a lot about the respect that your new leader gives to those who were there before they were invited on board. An enlightened manager understands that they have to earn the respect of their extended team. They also realize that their success is dependent upon how their team perceives them as their leader. They can lose this respect on Day One if they choose to import their friends from the past and exclude their current staff without just cause for their actions. They may think they set the course of action through their vision and strategy, but it is the team below that executes the tactics that either make or break the overall effort. When this team is alienated by inappropriate hiring practices, the newly minted manager or executive has a tough road ahead and deservedly so. It's an ugly situation when the leader shouts "Take that hill!!" and looks back to see nobody behind him.

In any situation, when a plan goes awry, the great leader steps up, takes ownership, and then works to right the wrong. When it goes well, he is first to congratulate the people who did the real work and not take the credit for him or herself. Gifted leaders make decisions, and when these decisions are wrong, they make others based upon what was learned. They are focused on performance, measurement, and the analytics behind why outcomes happened as they did. They do not, however, stall out while they try to determine cause and effect. Leaders who are paralyzed by analysis are typically paranoid about failure. My late father-in-law, Don, was a senior executive at a major telecommunications corporation, who also had a distinguished career in the Armed Services. He worked as a Field Grade Officer (full Colonel) in command positions in NATO and at the Pentagon. Don knew a few things about leadership. One thing he taught me was that if you don't make mistakes, it means that you are not making decisions. Nobody makes all good decisions. Make a decision, learn from it, and then make another. He also taught that you need to make sure you don't make too many poor decisions, as that simply underlines that you are not qualified for the role you play. Keep that balance in perspective.

Great leaders are not afraid to make decisions. They are not paralyzed by analysis or lack of direction. They digest what is in front of them, and use the knowledge and the available tools to make a choice. When their judgment is not correct, they recognize the consequences of their initial action and make another decision to correct the error of their first choice. Decisions govern a temporary condition, and that condition can and will give way to another when a subsequent decision is made.

Your last step, therefore, is to scrutinize the quality of those decisions your management team makes. Do they make them quickly and decisively, or do they do the opposite? Decision paralysis perpetuates problems and causes opportunities to be lost. What is their leadership style, and how does it translate to success in the workplace? This has an impact on the company culture and also a large effect on the quality of the workplace environment. Do they make quality decisions that advance the organization's success, or do they all too often create additional obstacles by their choices?

As you improve, you will find that you are able to make valid determinations, and that you get better with practice. First, tightly define what decision you want to measure then gather the facts about its results. Finally, measure its impact on the business from organizational and customer points of view. When you are done, review your work and assign a resulting score to their work. Ensure that you eliminate hearsay and personal prejudice, and you should have a good picture that may offer surprising results.

These are just several of the questions you need to ask in order to place your management team in the proper perspective. None of it takes a considerable investment of your personal resources, and most of it can and should be done continuously in order to stay abreast of the current environment. The ultimate goal is to create your own sense of self-discipline so that this type of observation becomes second nature. I've been both negatively and positively surprised during my career as I dug into the background and habits of managers and senior execs in companies for which I've worked. This knowledge never hurt me, but often helped me make decisions that protected my career and also my family's well being. As in all other examples in this book, the more information about your job and organization that you are able to gather and digest, the closer you are to becoming an *Eyes Wide Open™* employee with a high level of awareness and preparedness.

Problem or solution?

Employers view their employees from a different perspective than how employees view each other. They look at their workers as how productive they are, and how capable they are at the completion of assigned work. The human element comes into the equation on a far lower level than the work level. From the employer's point of view, there are two types of employees: those who are part of the problems that are resident within the company, and the others who are part of the solution to the achievement of the organization's objectives. If you plan to remain with an employer, you need to determine which category you, your co-workers, management, and various others fall into. In order to get the most out of your job for both you and your employer, get involved and actively become part of the solution.

Employees who have been in positions for extended periods of time (for example, five years or more) are sometimes categorized as part of the organization's problem. This is especially true when they do not remain on the forefront of their trade or craft. These individuals frequently cling to the way things were done in the past, because change is painful and often threatens their status quo. Many have not changed in their thinking as the landscape around them transitioned from what it once was into what it is today. Others are simply less engaged in the business than those who have less tenure. Passion may also wane after several years of doing the same thing over and over.

I worked with an IT professional who was in charge of a large company's web infrastructure. When engaged in conversations about how the web site should be improved, he would spout, "I've been here for twelve years and know how it should work." That was the problem ... he had been there for twelve years and had lost vision, passion, and was out of touch with the modern approach to what used to be his specialty. He had become a dinosaur.

These individuals should be dealt with and either replaced entirely or rotated to fresh positions. This provides them with new responsibilities in order to re-invigorate their careers as well as their ability to contribute. The company of today is NOT the company that it was five years ago. The same strategy and tactics used in the past do not function at maximum efficiency and may not be relevant today.

On a personal level, when you find yourself in this category, you should perform a self review and determine if it is time to re-invent yourself. Obvious choices are to add a new skill or apply for a role in another department that will encourage you to expand your horizons and provide additional value to your employer. One of the goals of this book is to provide insights into how your involvement and proactive choices support your ability to secure and/or advance your career. If you read this and believe that you could be part of the problem, you have work to do.

Business _is_ personal

There is a myth that has been perpetrated over the years by the saying, "It's not personal. It's just business." Don't be mistaken—business is very personal. Don't kid yourself and think that it isn't. This saying is simply a crutch that gives the speaker an excuse for their behavior.

"It's not personal. It's just business" means several things, none of them good. The first possibility is that the person who utters the saying has either just delivered or is about to deliver bad news. This news may be spawned by company policy, and perhaps that person has not bought into it. The saying shifts responsibility for the news away from the messenger and to the company. This is another way of saying, "Don't shoot the messenger." An example of this is when a manager must lay someone off due to a reduction in force. A lost job is very personal.

It may also mean that the person who uses the phrase has a self-serving agenda without a sound basis. They may rely on these words to cloak their true intentions. It enables someone to act in a particular way, which is driven by selfish, personal motives. Have you ever heard this phrase followed up with something that was beneficial to the person to whom it was spoken? I doubt it, and believe this outcome is the drastic exception rather than the general rule.

There are cases, however, where actions could be driven by sound business reasons. An example might be a situation where someone needs to step up the speed with which they complete a cyclical task. This task could be, for example, submission of an order for release to the factory floor for completion. The need for increased speed does not originate from a personal perspective, but from a business need to move orders through the system faster. My experience, however, shows that the "Business, not personal" tactic is not the typical tactic that someone would use to shorten order release cycle times on a manufacturing floor. Other, less cryptic directions are more likely to be used in order to get the desired effect. These are much more straightforward with attention drawn to the need, followed by mutual agreement on the required outcome.

In any case, my advice here is to immediately go on "Red Alert" if and when you hear this phrase. It usually is not tied to a positive outcome. Since business is personal on many levels, this saying should sound like a fire alarm going off in your head.

Nice people don't pay my bills

There is a common comment heard at work that is usually similar to, "He is a nice guy but ... ." This phrase refers to people who may be pleasant, but who do not have the skills, knowledge, or experience to execute the job to which they are assigned. There are a lot of nice people in the world, but being nice does not translate to being a good employee, co-worker, or colleague. The results can be detrimental to your employment when you are paired with such a person on a project or task. You may be brought down to their level, unless you take the initiative to overcome their lack of input and choose to excel. Do not fall prey to the "Nice guy—bad co-worker" syndrome.

Learn to separate personal from business traits in employees, co-workers, and colleagues. Do not permit a positive or negative personality trait cloud your business judgment about an individual. Assessment of those around you should be part of how you conduct yourself at work. Know who you work for, who works for you, as well as whom you work with. This offers a layer of protection and also enables you to know how to leverage those around you in the completion of your assigned role. Leverage does not mean manipulate. Instead, it refers to know how to align resources to accomplish assignments or tasks.

I met many nice people at work during the different stops of my career. Some nice people were extremely skilled and talented, but others populated the other end of the spectrum. This latter group always gave me pause. It was okay to have an occasional lunch with them, but I never made it a habit. I often felt that they used their endearing qualities to overcome gaps in their abilities. This often left me with the feeling that I was being "gamed" by them. In other words, they had an ulterior motive in acting overly friendly, and tried to get ahead on style instead of substance.

POWERPOINT

LEARN FROM EVERYBODY

Everybody you encounter is a potential learning opportunity. The learning can be either positive or negative, but the fact is, what they have to offer should be learned and placed in your catalog of life experiences. Through your observation of others, you discover multiple items that should be added to your repertoire. Even if you observe the most offensive behavior, learn from it. Learn that it is offensive, and do not repeat it or do anything similar. When it is positive and fits into your character, adopt it or a version of the observed behavior, and use it to your best advantage.

Ensure that you are willing to learn lessons from others, even when they don't consciously offer them. People, in general, have a wealth of knowledge to share. It is an easy task to learn from them, provided you are open and accepting. It is a process that can range from a request to a mentor for assistance, to the observation of a colleague who makes a major faux pas in an important meeting. These examples and everything in between offer learning events that add to your real world education provided you keep your mind open to accept them.

Greed and Power

The desire for money and material possessions drives people to do things that hurt others, including you, unless you are alert and protect yourself. There is a reason Greed is one of the Seven Deadly Sins— it destroys its perpetrators and those around them. The havoc that is wrecks is not just perpetrated by C-level executives. It can also be found in co-workers, immediate management, mid-level executives, and even your customers.

At the highest levels of the organization, many public company executives receive compensation in addition to their base salary. These incentives are in the form of stock options and bonuses. Their bonus is typically based upon the achievement of top and bottom line financial performance. The value of their options is normally tied to stock price performance in the short to mid-term. The underlying option value increases when the stock price increases. This is corporate insanity at its finest, since it focuses on near team results and shifts attention from the long term strategy that must be in place for the company's continued health and growth. Decisions that the owners of these options make may be solely focused on the increase in value of their stock. Are these decisions always what are best for the company, its customers, and employees? The answer is that there absolutely must be a balanced approach in order to drive both short and longer term performance. The danger expressed here can be best illustrated by the words of a regional President of a global software company, "Why should I worry about what happens in two years. If I don't make my (sales) quota this quarter, I will be fired and won't have anything to worry about."

Private companies frequently travel on the road to become public traded as they seek to cash in on the capital available through a successful Initial Public Offering (IPO). Conversion to public status means a huge windfall of monetary gains for those individuals fortunate enough to be able to materially participate in the event. It is a common practice for private company executives to own a percentage of the company in one form or another. This percentage of ownership is converted to stock when the company goes public. This results in, perhaps, millions of dollars for those who are properly vested and who participate in the IPO. While this is not an indictment of the process, it is a notice that you, as an employee, should take note of executive behaviors during this period. Greed and self interest could drive decisions and activities that are not in the best interest of others. If you find yourself in this position, attempt to understand why company-related events happen, why decisions are made, and what the business or personal drivers of the leadership are that guide executive behaviors.

The lust for power is closely associated with those who are consumed by the pursuit of money. There is a library full of books written on this subject alone. Suffice it to say it is imperative that you remain vigilant for behaviors that are evidence of the lust for power. Again, this is not limited to those in management or executive levels. This trait may be possibly found in the co-worker who stands next to you or sits in the next cubicle or desk.

It is common for those who do not have much power over events in their personal lives to attempt to fill that void through the exertion of some measure of personal power through less than savory means at work. The caveat here is to be aware of what drives the actions of those around you, and realize character defects are not limited to any specific group. These are equal opportunity conditions that affect people from all walks of life, and unless you are vigilant, they can surprise you when you least expect. Two examples of this behavior at a personal level might be when you are shut out of a project, and when you purposefully do not receive an invitation to a key conference call that you should be invited to. While the effect may not have great impact upon you, it gives the person who commits the act a feeling of control—or power—over others.

Land grabbing and empire building

Internal dissonance destroys a company from the inside out. Even an enterprise with a superior product, good market position, current fiscal success, and all the indicators of good fortune can be undermined. All that is necessary is the infighting or self-serving actions of key individuals as they strive to forward their careers through self-aggrandizement and a culture of "Me, me, and me." When "me" becomes more important than "we," you can bet trouble is not far behind.

Empire building is a common and dangerous activity that promotes the agenda of an individual or group at the expense of the organization and its customers. It can happen everywhere throughout the organization from the individual to the Executive Boardroom level.

A common mid- level management example occurs when a manager hires staff in order to add headcount that is not necessary to accomplish the assigned work. These managers feel they gain additional power and clout in the organization when they have a larger team than their peers. This is expensive and deceptive. It can negatively affect people in that leader's chain of command, since they may find themselves in roles that are less fulfilling than those for which they were hired. This frequently happens when managers also engage in a land grab. This behavior should not be rewarded with a larger staff, but with a pink slip, a cardboard box, and directions to the exit door instead.

Land grabbing is similar in that a management level individual attempts to grab as much territory within the organization as they are able in order to increase their personal influence and power. They may not have the skills or bandwidth to manage their own area let alone the areas in question, but that does not hinder them from thoughtless efforts at expansion. Again, this behavior is unhealthy for the company as well as the resources involved. It must be identified, stopped, and consequences applied.

Your guidance is not to become involved in someone else's schemes and plans. An opportunity to move into such a group may look enticing on the surface, but under further scrutiny it becomes what it is … a staffing scheme to satisfy the ambitions of a misguided individual or group. If recruited for support for either of these schemes, the safest action is to remain unaligned. You may feel you are forced to take sides, but your best alternative is to remain neutral. Follow the facts and not your emotions in these situations, and know that you have alternatives to black or white. You have your job on which to focus and should not be distracted by someone else's plotting and scheming.

The Cast of Characters in the Theater of Work

A similar Cast of Characters is found in almost every organization with a sufficient number of employees to represent the different categories. Their names and faces may change as well as their physical appearance and gender. In the long run, though, you will find many representatives of the Cast of Characters at work next to you. You should consciously be aware of them, especially when you are transferred to a new department or take a position with another company. Throughout your career, you find the traits of those with whom you come into contact can be cross-referenced to others with whom you interacted or observed in the past. This is neither good nor bad. It is just a fact based upon observation. It should also be something to which you pay close attention, as this saves you time, energy, and, perhaps, other valuable assets as you navigate through the minefield of personalities you encounter. Work is real life drama played out in front of you every day. Know which part you play, and learn to play it well.

A number of different characters are noted in the pages that follow. This is not intended to be a complete list, but instead, its purpose is to get you to think about your personal cast of players. This way, you may open your eyes and be less surprised about those with whom you encounter on the stage called work. These individual types may appear as they are described below, or as a combination of two or more characteristics. One of the traits is usually the most dominant.

The Empty Suit: a waste of a good headcount slot

Perhaps you know a manager or executive (typically) who has little or no true business skill, but who is in a position to lead others and make significant decisions that affect the organization. Then you know an Empty Suit. The Empty Suit adds little value, due to lack of basic knowledge about business or the area of which they command. They don't provide clear direction and typically are driven by emotion rather than logic. Their lack of skill is blatantly transparent, and they tend to become exposed in a relatively short time. This doesn't mean that they go away or get removed, though. That would be too good to be true. Many times their lack of business savvy is masked by a bully-like or blustery persona. Similar to most schoolyard bullies, the Empty Suit readily backs down when confronted, since all they have is a thin veneer to mask their true abilities.

One of the traits of the Empty Suit is that they contribute nothing while they take up valuable space. Many Empty Suits may have never had an original thought in their life. When provided with a presentation, email, white paper, or project plan to review, the common answer from this person is, "Looks good to me" or "I agree." Instead of content revisions or meaningful edits, you are lucky to get more than comments on grammar and spelling. When assigned to a project, they wait for others to offer their input and quickly add "I agree" with what sounds best to them. They either have no opinion, or in those rare situations when they might, do not have the wherewithal to share it. This individual may be competent enough to hold their position if they are an individual contributor, but are never to be relied upon to provide added value to anything or anyone else. I once worked with a classic Empty Suit. He was quickly exposed, whereupon we took great pleasure to send items to him for comment because we knew what we would get in return. A case was built and presented to his manager who acted upon the information to remove him. Now the "Suit," as he became to be called, agrees as an assistant manager at a fast food chicken restaurant and not as a program manager at a global software company.

Fish Out of Water: out of their element

Some individuals are skilled, smart, and talented but are simply in the wrong role. Try as they might, they can't seem to get their hands around the job at hand and excel in their performance. For example, not all great sales people make good sales managers. Most task oriented people would not make good strategists. The list of examples is endless, and the toll this miscasting takes on the individual, department, and the organization is considerable.

These Fish Out of Water are products of poor hiring methodologies that do not match the correct individual with the right job. Job skills, experience, and personality profiles that need to be taken into account during the recruitment of new hires. Incorrect hiring methodologies and placement becomes expensive from both the human resource and investment points of view. When the employee fails, the investment of hiring and training them follows the departing individual out of the door.

There is a sub group of the Fish Out of Water known as the Incompetent. No matter what they do or how hard they try to do it, they are mismatched to the task at hand. Whether it is due to lack of skill, knowledge, experience, or innate intelligence, this person just does not meet the most minimum standards in whatever job they are assigned to perform. Recognize this fact, and if you manage them, do not fall into a trap and dole out unearned income through retention of them on your staff. If you are a co-worker, beware of their presence and potential impact. You may be expected to do what the Incompetent can't. There is no place for pity as you deal with this individual. They should be indentified and either moved to an area where they may somehow contribute, or fired so that they may find their place in the sun on someone else's payroll.

Welfare Recipient: hiding out yet collecting a salary

This seems to be a person more often found in large enterprise corporations. This is due to the fact that the larger an organization becomes, the more places it provides in which marginal people can hide. Corporate welfare recipients add absolutely no value to the organization, but seem to be kept on staff despite their lack of contribution. They represent the fact that corporations actually do offer welfare to select individuals.

You often find that Welfare Recipients are shuffled among departments and seemingly housed in the corporate equivalent of public housing. They seem to be adept at remaining on the payroll with a clear conscience. Beware of this individual. Ultimately, someone is watching them and is poised to remedy the situation. Guilt by association did not become a cliché because it was a lie.

The Weather Reporter: sunny with a chance of …

Another sub-species of Non-Contributors in the workplace is the Weather Reporter. When asked to offer a recap of a project or work item in a staff meeting, this colleague typically sounds as if they are the weather person on TV who reads how the weekend will be. They take input from their staff and read it without truly knowing the material. They parrot what others provide, and are not able to tie it into the business when pressed for a more detailed analysis. When asked, the oft quoted reply is usually, "I'll have to get back to you on that." This provides them with the ability to go back to someone else one more time for another weather report that they can subsequently read to you in order to mask their lack of under-standing of the question. The best course of action when you want accurate information is to circumnavigate the Weather Reporter, and go directly to their staff.

The Workaholic: treading water and going nowhere fast

They come in early and eat in place at their desks. They stay late and take work home. They are the Workaholics who never get off the treadmill. Many of us work hard and long for defined periods of time out of necessity, but this type never relents. Vacations? Rarely are they taken. Family? A distant second place. The reasons for the way they act are varied yet understandable. Workaholics may seek rec-ognition for whatever reason. They may believe this is the way they advance up the corporate ladder. Workaholics may exhibit a sense of paranoia due to low self esteem or simply not enough skill to match their position. They may believe the extra time on the job may over-come their deficiency. Lack of self-confidence is typically masked by a false bravado and often a self-important manner. This is the person for whom the phrase "Get a life!" was invented. The sad observation about the Workaholic is that they never seem to advance or make considerably more money in exchange for what they forego, as they dedicate their life to the grind. They are the human equivalent of gerbils on a wheel.

Empire Builder: greed and low self esteem

"I need more people." "I don't have enough resources." Both of these quotes are the native cries of the Empire Builder. This individual embodies all that is wrong with this trait. The Empire Builder looks to gain power through an increase in staff—often staff that should not report to them under any circumstances, or other times, staff that is oversized for their mission. It often does not end with building a bloated team. They also attempt to seize control of other areas of the business in order to extend their reach.

This has the potential to result in many things, none of which is positive. First and foremost, they look out for themselves above all others. This means you could be in their Inner Circle and still be an afterthought. The Empire Builder may not have the skills required to run a larger team or business unit, which places the team and the company in jeopardy. They are known to fudge statistics that bend reality in order to build a case that gets them closer to their personal goals. These are dangerous people.

These individuals often measure their self-worth by the job roles, number of direct reports, and the size of the staff they personally control. Their low self esteem is massaged through the addition of headcount or responsibilities. Beware of this self-aggrandizing behavior, and do not get swept up in their plans to rule the world.

The Beige people: always below the radar

This is the average or just below average contributor: never good enough to promote, but not poor enough to eliminate from the team. This person never takes a risk, always flies below the radar, produces enough work to not be noticed, and never stands out enough to be seen in either a positive or negative light. They typically have just enough of a spark to add to the overall value of the team with which he or she works, but never enough to start a fire. Color this person "Beige."

The Beige employee is found more often in larger organizations where they can hide and their lack of initiative and contribution can be masked to a greater degree. They are exposed readily in smaller, vibrant businesses where everyone is 100% focused and engaged at all times. These individuals' lack of spark can reduce the productivity of whatever group with which they are associated. Beware of these people. They have little to offer, and their mediocrity can become a disease. If you are a manager, weed them out mercilessly, since they are not worth the time you need to invest in them. No amount of training can advance them from a "C" to "A" status.

The Connected Individual: family or personal ties

This person can be either an asset or a liability. It depends upon their character and the quality of the skills they possess. This is the individual who personally knows someone in a prominent position in your employer's hierarchy, via a business connection or through a relation—cousin, uncle, brother, sister, etc. They may or may not have earned their position and often feel protected due to ties to someone high in the food chain. This doesn't mean that they aren't quality individuals. They did not choose to whom they are related. They must, however, be judged on their own merits. At their best, they can be a great organizational asset, since their connections may give them Inner Circle connections, which tend to get things done and done quickly. At their worst, they can damage whatever they touch and frequently leverage a sense of empowerment spawned by their connections. You usually won't find the Connected Individuals at the head of the line to get pink slips in a downturn. Their connections give them a degree of insulation, but not total immunity.

Golden Boy - or Girl: a star is born

This is the co-worker who can do no wrong. This title often has negative connotations, but it can be positive as well. Golden People are either connected, have excelled while they executed an important task, manage upward very well, or are just plain good. Whatever the reason, they are pure gold in the eyes of management. This label should not summarily be considered negative, since some Golden People leverage this status to the best advantage of the company, their co-workers, and themselves, of course. An enlightened individual recognizes their advantage and leverages it to advance items that are beneficial to the business. When they do this, their peers embrace them as they see a collective benefit. Beware, however. The opposite is frequently very, very true. It all depends upon the ego of the individual in question. A self-absorbed Golden Person can wreck havoc on morale and the performance of those around them. Do not be quick to judge, but, rather, be alert and aware of how this person handles their mantle. A Golden Person of good character does the opposite and can potentially be a personal as well as a company asset.

Closely related to the Golden Person is Today's Star. Are they a one hit wonder or is their recent success an indicator of good things to come? Look around. You probably notice this individual. They come from pools of people who have recently excelled and whose accomplishments have been noticed. Members of this group may choose to wear this mantle of recognition in several ways: they either show humility and strive to improve further, or let their ego detract from past accomplishments through braggadocio. How people handle themselves when they achieve significant things is a window into their character.

When you personally accomplish something significant, ensure that you graciously accept the acknowledgement, share it as appropriate with other contributors, and enjoy the moment. After your brief personal victory dance, immediately look to your next objective. Use it as a driver to take you to the next subsequent step on your journey.

The Dreamer: pie in the sky

Wishes do not make dreams happen, and gold mines do not fall out of the sky. Dreamers are just that—co-workers who imagine they will accomplish things, but who do little that is necessary to get them to their destination. Dreamers excel at lunchroom fantasies while they eat their baloney sandwiches. Their plans are built on fantasies that save the company, the planet, and the whales, but there is one catch ... their imaginary schemes never get put into action. Dreamers are different from Achievers in one major way—they dream, hypothesize, plan, plot, and scheme, but do not put action plans into motion and achieve anything. Their hot air may be a measurable contributor to global warming.

Contrarian: totally out of the box

Most people think in a similar fashion when faced with similar situations. A Contrarian marches to their own drummer, and processes information from a unique angle that is all their own. This offers a different perspective than the majority offers, which is neither good nor bad—just different. These colleagues should be recognized for what they are because they can either be a disruptive liability or a valuable "out of the box" asset. When the Contrarian makes suggestions that are not main stream and are so out of the ordinary that they can't work, they need to understand why. Their defining moment is when they agree to accept this or not. If they understand that some of their ideas and thoughts are simply too contrary to the norm, we simply move on. If, on the other hand, they do not, they can prove to be an obstacle that must be dealt with. Contrarians who offer a point of view that is out of the norm and productive are valuable in the sense that their minds go where others' do not. This can often lead to new solutions. You, as a colleague, must be able to accept, filter, and process the Contrarian's offerings. This is especially true in situations where their unique perspective may provide benefit to a project or other work item.

The Bull Dog: death grip on their "bone"

This person is either issue or task focused and attacks the job with tunnel vision. They latch onto something and simply will not let go until it's done—usually to <u>their</u> satisfaction. Beware! This is not always a positive trait, as it can get in the way of true progress. Success in today's world often demands multi-tasking and team work. This bull dog demeanor can lead to a narrow focus, which limits one's ability to contribute. They also tend to snare co-workers in their net of single-mindedness, and limit the productivity of others with whom they work.

The Bull Dog commandeers assistance from where ever they can. They expect their highest priority to be yours as well and therein lays the problem. You may only have casual interest in the outcome of their project, but to them it is the entire earth and sky. This divergence of opinion lays the ground work for conflict that could cause problems.

The Achiever: can do

Think, plan, act, and achieve. This person is the one who can always be counted on to get things done. They complete what is given them to do, and usually ask for more. This trait can be combined with some of the others listed, much to the benefit of everyone concerned. The conclusion is that, through whatever means they employ, they get things done, and they get them done correctly. Their goal is their target, and their mission is focused on the achievement of that goal.

Achievers are a small minority of the population. They possess the traits necessary to accomplish their goals, and stop at little to cobble together support for their cause. These individuals may or may not personally possess the skills and knowledge needed to accomplish their purposes, but know how to enlist the support of those who do. Organizations are fortunate to have these employees on staff. They may be found everywhere from the lowest to the highest levels of the organization, and are usually on the move due to their drive for achievement.

The Senator: builds a flawless coalition

This individual walks the halls and gains individual consensus before they propose their ideas or initiatives to a wider audience. He or she is very good at gathering support for initiatives and programs that they wish to see come to fruition. They make consensus-building an organic part of how they do business. Senators do not win through the application of brute force, but through the art of presentation and skillful persuasion. While not always found at the executive level, the executive-level Senator is the most visible of this breed by the nature of their position. Their presence should generally be welcomed, since their behavior is a respectful way to draw attention to an issue and to reach approval for action plans on a one-to-one basis. They are usually a positive force with the common good foremost in their mind. Senatorial behavior should be learned if it is not innate. It is not an easy skill to master, and takes considerable practice. Those who consciously adopt it are made to think through the issues they champion before they begin to build their coalition. This forces them to substantiate their position on a proactive basis if they are to find success. These are generally persuasive people who passionately believe in what they promote. This gives them an advantage as their conviction alone sways many who sit on the fence of indecision.

Future CEO: on the move

There are very few of these in the workplace. In fact, you may only meet one or two in a career, but when you do, they stand out as the future stars they may become. These individuals are well rounded, intelligent, well read, possess a high degree of integrity, and are natural born leaders. They can quickly size up complex situations, and arrive at an understanding that enables them to make decisions that are beneficial and productive. These stars are hard working, smart people who know how to produce results no matter what task is placed before them.

Future CEOs are great people to observe and to learn from, since they possess the qualities most respected in business. One word of caution is that they can lose their way if their work takes over and dominates their personal life. This is not a trait to imitate, but instead it is a trait to identify and avoid. The loss of this balance causes a lack of focus and conflict between both work and personal responsibilities.

Summary

What has been offered above is a short cut to the recognition of similarities among co-workers. Do not, however, let it turn into a screening exercise that includes or excludes people based solely on these observations. To ignore someone because of a self-generated label is not healthy to your career nor is it fair to the individual. Take the high road and learn how to work with a broad range of personality and character types based on who they are and the value they provide. Understand that you will meet recurring types of individuals on the job.

Certain traits are common and appear repeatedly in the people you encounter over the years. Know this and use it to assist you to recognize behaviors that may be a help or hindrance.

READINESSREVIEW

When I state that you should work with your Eyes Wide Open™, my intent is that you not only do a great job at the tasks to which you are assigned, but also possess an awareness of whom you work for and with. This recipe for success is a blend of many ingredients that are learned and honed over a period of time. The secret sauce is to know what the ingredients are, so that you are able to use them appropriately and then improve your associated skill levels as you grow.

This chapter offers insights into the people you encounter in the work place. You learned that they are not just the warm bodies that you see every day, but that they have varying degrees of impact on you. Some are beneficial, while others are obstacles. Others are inert with respect to you and your career. The goal here is not to encourage you to hang labels on people, but to open your eyes to the fact that you need to have a high level of awareness about your environment in order to be the most efficient and effective at what you do. This enables you to, as the U.S. Army recruiting saying states, "Be all that you can be."

PERSONAL DEVELOPMENT ACTIONS

- Identify the individual with whom you would love to play golf with, but who adds absolutely nothing on the job. Do you avoid or engage them knowing that their contributions may be limited? What other possibilities are there for different types of interactions?

- Remember a colleague who was always seen as a problem rather than a solid contributor. What was the reason for this reputation? How could they have become part of the solution rather than continuing as part of the problem? How are you viewed? If the view is neutral, would you consider this healthy? List three ways that establish you as a source for solutions.

- Perform a review of everyone with whom you work on a regular basis. Who contributes to your work and who represents an obstacle? Who are your allies who may not be in the group with whom you regularly associate? Who can be relied upon to put in the quality effort needed for either you or your team to accomplish goals? Do you need to build additional bridges to others? Take the randomness out of work associations and interact with a purpose without being overtly self-serving.

- Identify the public image of your organization's leadership. Does this match how they actually act and perform in the execution of their roles? While the workplace may be a stage, the players should remain true to their character and not display different faces for different situations. When you observe inconsistencies in how management acts in order to serve their best interests, beware. Something is not right and caution should be taken.

- Perform a background check on your employer's leadership. Even though you may not be a research analyst, tools are available and at your disposal. Find out where they came from, what their qualifications are, and how well matched they are to the current business conditions of your organization. Review their most recent projects and proposals to determine the current direction they are steering. A passive attitude with respect to your organization's direction makes you no more than a passenger on a cruise ship without an itinerary. You know it is headed somewhere, sometime, and think you will do something along the way. You would not sign up for that trip,

CHAPTER FIVE
YOU AND YOUR MANAGER

This relationship may be the number one factor which determines if you are or are not satisfied with your job. It can keep you happily employed or drive you to seek other opportunities. When it is not healthy, it can cause issues both at work and at home that have the potential to disrupt an otherwise happy existence. Your relationship with your manager can provide opportunities for fulfillment and advancement. It can make getting up in the morning and preparing for work a happy experience you look forward to each and every day.

Doesn't it stand to reason, therefore, that you should focus a considerable amount of time and energy on your relationship with your manager? You become a more informed person when you cultivate that relationship. Much guess work is eliminated because you get it from the source and not through the grapevine. In the longer term, you gain more control of your life, since you understand the current state of your relationship with them. When you understand your supervisor, you also are more knowledgeable about how to more effectively manage your relationship with them. Lack of knowledge means lack of understanding. Any time you lack an understanding of someone, you tend to deal with them emotionally and not objectively, since you don't have a grasp of their point of view. This relegates you to a reactive position as you attempt to understand them after the fact, rather than prior to the event.

A positive relationship with your manager that is based upon mutual respect is the ideal, although it isn't possible one hundred per cent of the time. There are, however, steps you can take that permit you to get more from the relationship than if it is not nurtured. This chapter uncovers many of these points for you to consider. Should you choose to weave them into the fabric of your work, you will be more prepared to create a plan to manage your relationship with the individual who supervises you. If you choose otherwise, you expose yourself to the random acts that result from a lack of preparation and planning.

The scope of your relationship with your manager is complex. They want to advance to the next level, just as you do. Their team members want their job, and often believe they could do it much better. There are constant pressures to achieve goals and objectives. Their training is typically minimal, and guidance from above very spotty. They must manage a wide variety of personalities and skills. Most importantly, they must be leaders to whom others look to follow in order to achieve what must be accomplished.

Take the appropriate amount of time to arrive at an understanding of your manager's position and the person they are. You may be surprised at what you discover. They are also human. What you learn may change your relationship with them for the benefit of all concerned.

Your manager's focus

You may or may not like your manager or have a good relationship with them, but have you ever stopped for a minute to understand why? Your manager is a real person with both personal and professional lives. They have pressures that come from all angles that are much different than those you face on the job. Their priorities are aligned with those of their team, but they are viewed through a manager's lens and not that of a team member. Managers have a personal life and career aspirations along with the demands that accompany both. In short, managers are human, and need a certain amount of understanding if you are to prosper under their command.

Managers and other types of bosses may not communicate well enough to let you know what is important to them. They may not properly express their goals and objectives, since effective communication is not a widely developed and leveraged skill today in the managerial ranks. Therefore, it is incumbent upon you to uncover what is important to your boss. This lets you know some baseline items that must be included in your list of how you support him or her. This exercise becomes much the same thing as a sale based upon the Needs Analysis methodology: how is your manager measured, what keeps them up at night, what would your manager like to see that would deliver improved results, and what are their pain points? Once you know these answers, you are in a better position to align your efforts to your manager's needs and increase your chances for an improved relationship.

There should always be sensitivity to those areas of the business that are most important to them. This ensures that cooperation and teaming becomes more pronounced and productive. Things that are important to your boss must be important to you as well, especially at your review time. Your production is an important factor if you are to receive a positive review. The possibilities for a good result are dramatically increased when you are in harmony with your manager.

Once you realize your manager is a person with career goals, production pressures, and the responsibility to lead their team effectively, you have insight into how they think and behave. This is your next step toward productive alignment with your manager and places you on the way to a better understanding of how to leverage this relationship to your advantage—and to theirs, as well.

POWERPOINT

THE CHAIN OF COMMAND

Organizations have a Chain of Command for a reason. The members of the chain are in place to facilitate the orderly cascade of vision, mission, strategy, and tactics from the boardroom to the company floor and back again. Respect for the Chain of Command is essential. Leap frogging over multiple levels in the Chain of Command is not a business strategy; it is a recipe for disaster.

Communication up the Chain should begin with contact with your immediate manager. In cases where you feel a need to communicate to an authority that ranks above your supervisor, it is a good idea to initially work through them to gain access to those above. If they are unresponsive, attempt a second time, and document appropriately. If this fails, either work through HR (in situations suitable to HR), or set an appointment with your manager's manager. It is imperative that you demonstrate repeated attempts were made to leverage your direct manager, but failed. You do not have to cast a negative light on them in order to do so, but their boss should know the attempts were made. Consistently measure your actions against the issues they may potentially create, and the benefits they might deliver.

Manage your manager

Many companies make a common mistake and promote individuals into managerial roles because of their superior performance in the role they are now expected to manage. The belief is that the proper career path for high performers is to manage those who have the same job as they previously held. Is it a safe assumption that a top producing sales executive has the skills and tools to manage a team of sales agents effectively? Are the skills, experience, knowledge, and aptitude the same for both roles? The answers are "No" to both Does the knowledge of corporate financials, for example, produce a good finance department manager? The answer falls much closer to "No" than "Yes" because, while the manager needs financial knowledge, they also need to have the skills and aptitude required to manage people. It is, there-fore, imperative that you appraise your manager to determine their skill level in the execution of their role as both a people manager and as a role manager. If they were promoted due to their past perform-ance in their job role, they may have gotten to where they are due to a bad promotion decision that was actually beyond their control. They might be great individual contributors, but sadly unprepared for man-agement.

In my experience, I found that most managers can't effectively manage. This is typically not their fault. The cause is frequently their organization's poor promotion practices, which are then exacerbated by a lack of management training. It is also, in some cases, the fact that the manager lacks the aptitude required for success on the job. Often times a new manager is given their title, a desk, and nothing more. I, for example, was once promoted to the position of National Sales Director for a division of a two billion dollar technology company. The company prepared me by supplying a team of twelve sales reps, a desk, stapler, pencil, notepad, and a phone. No training, orientation, or manual. Not even a customer list or relevant phone numbers. Our group succeeded, due not so much to my managerial skills, but to the decision of a great group of sales people (emphasis on "people") to get involved and collectively achieve our group's objectives. Through their support of me, they supported the company as well as themselves. I was simply the conduit through which it flowed.

Through understanding your manager's strengths and weaknesses, your relationship can be dealt with to everyone's best advantage. Help them help themselves, and in the process you help yourself. All of us, including our managers, have strong and weak points. It is vital that you lend a critical eye in order to understand their capabilities and limita-tions. Get to know where they excel and where they need help. My sales team in the previous paragraph did just that. Through our com-bined efforts, a solid team was built that leveraged the best of what each of us had to offer. This doesn't mean that they walked up to me and stated, "I am going to help you with xyz." On the contrary, they worked with me to identify where I needed assistance. Their offer of assistance went a long way to create a productive relationship.

This example demonstrates how you assume an active part in the administration of the relationship and not just be a passive bystander. Done properly, this is often identified as being "self-managed." In reality, you are actually acting as a mature, responsible employee who values their own time as well as their contribution to the organization. This is also characteristic of people who realize the best ideas do not always flow from the top down.

When you are a manager, you may also manage your own manager through participation in the planning process for the work that you and your team are expected to perform. Ensure that timelines and expectations are reasonable. Demonstrate your support for items upon which you agree. Appropriately push back when excessive demands are made of your team's time as well as your own. Some bosses thoughtlessly heap work on subordinates until pushback occurs. For some, this is a management style, albeit not a good one. For others, it could be that they are swept up in the moment and do not pay enough attention to detail. In any case, you can be the buffer between bad management and your team, and it is your responsibility to act accordingly.

Whether you are a manager or a member of a team, you must always have clarity related to what you need from your supervisor. This means identification of what you require for your personal success on the job. This should include a simplified gap analysis that lists what you need versus what is offered and available. This provides a logical view of any delta (the difference between what is and what should be) that may exist, and can be the basis for a productive conversation with your manager. This should then progress to an agreement related to how to work with them to fill the gap and secure what you need. Some managers may take offense at this type of approach, but others who are more enlightened should welcome the dialog. These do what they can to offer support that is within reason, and within their power to provide.

Following is a partial list of examples of queries that should be addressed during this process:

- Did your manager set proper expectations for job performance for you? If not, then it is your responsibility to obtain them. Don't wait because it may not happen.

- Do you have the tools and training that enable your success? If not, do you know how to obtain them or do you need your manager's assistance to do so?

- Do you know how your performance is measured? Some organizations use scales such as "Needs Improvement," "Meets Expectations" and "Exceeds Expectations" while others use alpha or numeric scales to measure performance. Do you know your employer's methodology and how these are defined relative to your position?

- Do you understand the nominal career path attached to your position? Do you have the Job Description for the next position you aspire to? If not, it is your responsibility to secure the information, since it is your career. Set an appointment with a specific agenda that covers this need. Hold your manager accountable for what they should provide to you.

- Did you receive your periodic review on time? If not, schedule it yourself—don't wait and complain later. Become action oriented when you work with managers. Do not allow them to overlook you.

It is difficult to understand why organizations have so few manager's handbooks or manuals to guide them through the challenging role that is people management. They seem to assume that elevation to a role that requires professional and interpersonal skills automatically includes the mystical acquisition of these competencies. I am continually astonished by how many companies have new hire training, remedial employee training, and additional curricula to develop the rank and file employee, but have the equivalent of empty shelves for manager training. Do not assume that your manager has the skills, knowledge, and experience to guide you in all phases of leadership, career guidance, and professional development. In fact, this is the exception. Therefore, if you are to be successful, you often have to "manage your manager."

Manage up, down and sideways

It is important to realize the need to manage in all directions in an organization. Whether you are a manager or not, you must learn to manage relationships with others, and not simply be the passive bystander who hopes things work out for the best. Learn how to operate at multiple levels and departments throughout your employer, and don't forget your peer relationships as well. As a manager, this includes your fellow managers who operate in the same level as you. The relationships you consciously build across the organization provide insight into what is happening outside of your immediate field of vision. Too much concentration on your own team results in tunnel vision and missed opportunities to exert influence on topical events.

Your active participation in relationships with your manager, team mates, peers, and others allows you to have a voice in many areas that affect you. This may not be something that you are comfortable with at first. As you continue to practice, your skills will improve as will your effectiveness. You may initiate this behavior through your demonstration of inquisitiveness about particular topics. Ask questions that show your interest in the business. Keep them simple at first so that you can build your knowledge and understanding. This eventually gets you into conversations where your point of view can be expressed. Through this course of action you may begin to influence others, including your manager.

There are two key points to this topic. The first is to choose to be involved. The choice to work in a vacuum does nothing to promote your self-interests and may make you a victim, since you abdicate your ability to influence or control anything. The second point is to be selective in what you choose to become involved with. Nobody appreciates someone with an overly vocal opinion on everything. This behavior dilutes your effectiveness. Choose your moments and be prepared to state your point of view on what is important to you. These guidelines apply to interactions with peers, managers, and subordinates. While you have to manage in all directions, you must do it wisely and judiciously.

Ally yourself to the right manager

Be aware of office politics. Someone's star is always in ascent while someone else's is headed earthward. It is a good idea to keep abreast of the change of direction related to those with whom you work, as these will eventually have either a direct or peripheral effect on you. This does not mean you become an office gossip, but rather it translates into your need to be an aware and informed person. This is just one more example of the necessity to know happens beyond your own personal world at work. You never want to be caught by surprise and it takes effort to ensure that you won't. I've seen entire teams decommissioned as a result of their manager's poor leadership and lack of political savvy. These people had to find new jobs within the organization within a thirty day period and were forced to scramble furiously to keep their paychecks intact. In this instance, only a single member of a team of twenty plus understood the politics at hand. They were insightful enough to leave that team and secure a new role before the purge began. Others had no idea and were caught in the mass scramble for survival.

A critical part of being aware and informed is to gain an understanding of your manager's relationship with others at equal or higher positions within the organization. Pay attention to how they conduct themselves in the presence of others in authority. Measure how they disseminate information to you and your team. Listen to what is being said about them without becoming a gossip yourself. Are they respected or not? Are they in ascension in their career path or going in the opposite direction? What is their skill level and background? These and similar observations are often critical to your future as you are associated with your supervisor, since you are part of their team. This association will eventually affect you to some degree, and if you do not like what you find, you have work to do.

You may wish to change positions within your organization when you are not satisfied with what you discover during your investigation. When you decide to change positions or roles within your company, do not just look at the desired position, but look at the management of the group of which you will be part of. You should build the same level of understanding about your potential manager as was discussed in the paragraph above relative to your current manager. This review must be one of the checkpoints that needs covered before you make your decision to change.

Your relationship with your manager is a major factor in job satisfaction. They are the conduit for information, career advancement, training, and a host of other job related items. They lead you or impede you. Your personal relationship with them is a source of satisfaction or stress. Ally yourself with the correct manager, and your life at work has the potential for success that the alternative cannot provide.

Inner Circles, Outer Circles

Leaders at every level of business have a select Inner Circle of associates whom they trust and listen to above all others. This group is responsible for the majority of the proposals that the leader considers for action. They are the group to whom the leader turns for counsel and feedback. These are the trusted few who have gained their positions due to a shared history of some combination of loyalty, achievement, and success.

Rarely do ideas from outside of the Inner Circle get onto their table for consideration. The exceptions are proposals that originate from someone outside of the Inner Circle, which are presented either through or by an Inner Circle member. This member acts as the proposal's Champion or Influencer. You may employ this route to get your ideas considered when you are faced with being shut out, because you are not connected well enough to get direct access to the Inner Circle.

This does not mean the proposal is a lock to be accepted, but it does get it into consideration. This illustrates how important it is to be aware of the political landscape that surrounds you at work. To some, it may be a confusing maze, but when you are informed, it is a tool which can be leveraged to your own best advantage. It is imperative to know the players and the roles they play.

While these may appear to be bold and sweeping generalizations, I found them to be true during years of experience. When you stop and think about how this applies to your own situation, who do you listen to the most? It is probably a few select friends and/or relatives … your own personal Inner Circle.

The political ecosystem becomes even more complex in many organizations. The larger an organization, the more possibilities arise for complexity. One of these complexities is a second layer that surrounds the leader—their Outer Circle. The Outer Circle is typically broader than the Inner Circle, but still limited in size. Smaller organizations may only have an Inner Circle, since their population does not support a secondary group. Also, a "Circle" may be one or two individuals. It does not have to be a larger group.

A two thousand member marketing group, of which I was a member, had a very private and limited Inner Circle of three individuals who had access to the Chief Marketing Officer (CMO). They actually had no official title or defined function tied to their Inner Circle role. It was an ad hoc group, but it was widely known that they were the CMO's trusted advisors. They were people with whom the CMO felt comfortable and with whom he had long and successful relationships. He also had his Marketing Leadership Group (MLG). This group fluctuated between seven to nine members. The size varied due to normal corporate personnel changes. This was his official staff that consisted of department heads and other functional leaders. They comprised his Outer Circle.

While the Outer Circle (his MLG) met weekly on a scheduled basis to formally discuss the issues related to the business, the Inner Circle met on an informal, as needed basis. They were the core team that created the company position on key issues, which were then placed on the agenda for the regular MLG meetings for action. These informal Inner Circle discussions were never open to others, unless by invitation.

The point to recognize here is to know who plays what role if you are to leverage any Circle-related relationships to your best advantage. This is step one. When you don't have relationships, you must begin to nurture and build them. This is a perfect opportunity to work with a purpose and not simply by chance. Your effort to build bridges does not have to only be with senior executives, but rather, it can—and should— begin with your immediate manager. Start locally and then expand as appropriate. Plan your actions with forethought to give yourself an edge over anyone who does not see what is beyond the surface. Don't shy away from the proposal of an appropriate idea to a Circle member. An option is to leverage your manager to address the appropriate Circle member with you. They are also helpful when they assist you to organize your thoughts for effective presentation. While this is not something that you should do too often, it may be done selectively with positive results. This way, you are not seen as a pest, but someone who has ideas who wants to contribute.

No surprise, no problem

You should take all necessary steps to make sure that your manager is never surprised by news that they should have heard first from you. Whether good or bad, you must keep them informed and in the loop, so that they are up-to-date on news and events of which you have knowledge.

Your manager represents you as well as your entire department to the rest of the organization. They need the most recent information, data, news, and current events if they are to execute their role properly. They make decisions based upon information they have at hand. When it is either incomplete or dated, their ability to execute is diminished and, potentially, your entire department suffers. In addition, it is an embarrassment for a manager to be caught unaware and to not be in possession of information that they should know. When the source of this missing information is you, it reflects negatively upon you and has the ability to damage a relationship that is a key to your career success.

A technician at a computer chip manufacturing company had knowledge about a production machine in the manufacturing process which displayed intermittent problems. This had the potential to interrupt local production and cause a stoppage along the entire manufacturing line. This is severe when you consider that these production lines must run 24 x 7 to be profitable due to the immense amount of capital that must be invested in equipment and associated infrastructure. Production stoppages have immediate, negative impact on profitability. The technician did not let his manager know of the issue, and instead worked with his immediate colleagues in an attempt to remedy the problem.

The technician's manager went into the weekly production meeting unaware of the issue. The meeting was chaired by the Vice President of Manufacturing who heard about the problem through his contacts and brought it up as a topic at the meeting. The manager was embarrassed in front of this VP as well as his peers because of his lack of knowledge of this potentially severe situation. To his credit, he assumed responsibility and immediately launched a corrective action effort. He also lost all confidence in the employee who should have kept him informed. This employee eventually transferred to another department. All of this could have been avoided if he simply spoke up and gave his manager vital information, so that he did not have to hear it from another source ... especially a department executive.

Attach remedies to problems

When you listen to people talk amongst themselves at work, you hear complaint after complaint about problems, but very little discussion about their effective solutions. The identification of a problem without an accompanying suggestion is nothing more than whining, and nobody likes a whiner! It is easy to find fault even with the best run organizations, since perfection in business does not exist. What separates the great from the not so great organizations is that the great ones don't just identify problems, they solve them. This begins with their employees. They depend upon their individual employees to both identify issues and provide suggestions for their solutions. This is a variant of the continuous improvement cycle that benefits the employees and customers as well.

Everyone has a complaint and can find fault, but not everyone can solve problems. The employees, being closest to the front line work that is performed, are usually the best at the identification of challenges and their possible solutions. It stands to reason that a successful company thrives when it listens to its employees' remedies to the issues they face in the performance of their duties. The best organizations solicit complaints with remedies from the employee base. They have mechanisms in place to recognize those contributions that make a difference to the health of the company and to the satisfaction of its customers.

You should bring problems and solutions to the table at the same time when you want to be heard, gain respect, and make true contributions. If your solution is not thought through and prepared for discussion, it is best to keep it to yourself. It is not ready to be shared. Your solution does not have to be documented to the Nth degree, but simply outlined in a manner that illustrates you have a grasp of the situation. It should also demonstrate that your proposal for improvement is plausible.

Management hears complaints about problems on a regular basis. They are often aware of the issues, and those who bring up complaints may simply re-state the obvious. This should not deter you, since your suggested solution may be the one that actually solves the common problem. Ensure that you always and without exception offer a suggested solution (or more than one) along with your observations about a problem. Always clearly state the topic you wish to address, and suggest how it can be realistically alleviated. Include risks associated with your suggestion as well as any known cost that may be incurred. This differentiates you from the masses, and also benefits the organization through the provision of a direction that might solve the issue.

POWERPOINT

CONSTANTS AND VARIABLES

When you look at a project, notice that the items that comprise it are divided into two groups: those which are Constant and do not change, and the others, which are Variable and may change due to circumstances.

Constants are often difficult to deal with because of their nature. You can spend an inordinate amount of time in an attempt to change them with little or no success. This wastes valuable resources and can frustrate or even defeat an individual or team. The best path forward here is to accept that they are Constants and organize your efforts with this fact in mind.

Variables, on the other hand, are changeable by nature. They can be altered from their current state, and ultimately may be made to be more useful, acceptable, or productive. This is where the bulk of your effort should be placed in order to obtain the maximum return. The decision about which to attack is similar to a decision to move either a rock as large as a car, or one as big as your toaster. One rock's size makes it obviously Constant while the other is Variable.

The application of the proper balance of available resources against the Constants and Variables reduces frustration and increases productivity. It is imperative that you recognize the nature of the items against which your efforts are applied so that you spend your time on the most productive pursuits. This is especially valuable when those resources are restricted and timelines are tight.

Lack of experience

Some of us just "haven't been there and haven't done that." We lack the experience that is only earned through the past execution of a particular task or role. Mistakes or errors in judgment are sometimes made that are spawned by our exposure to a new situation, and not due to a deficit of good judgment or common sense. Experience is a great teacher. It allows us to leverage items previously learned to more competently perform our jobs.

When you are a new employee or find yourself in a new position, you are exposed to unfamiliar situations that are common to your new role. How you handle these situations is critical to your development as well as the organization's success. Left alone without capable management, this means you may make more errors than someone would make with equal intelligence, ability to reason, and experience.

This is where a good management system comes into play. Skilled managers assist those new to positions in order to make them proficient in their roles in the shortest period of time. Common pitfalls are pointed out so they may be avoided. Proven techniques that drive productivity are shared. This minimizes the effects of the new employee's lack of experience and condenses the time required to make them fully productive. On the other hand, the inverse is true. Poor managers do not properly assist new subordinates and the common new hire mistakes occur. This ends up as a "lose-lose" situation for the employee, manager, organization, and, possibly the customer.

This is why it is imperative that you know the experience and skill level of your manager so that you can leverage their experience to your best advantage. When you are new to their team, this may be difficult, since you don't know what you don't know. You need to pay close attention to them and observe their actions in order to make a value judgment, since their competency can affect your progress. You may have to be somewhat aggressive in order to get what you need. When they do not offer suggestions willingly, you have to pull the information out of them. In situations where they simply are devoid of the knowledge you seek, you have to tactfully look elsewhere and get what is required for your personal success.

POWERPOINT

FOCUS ON THE LITTLE THINGS

Keep this anecdote in mind: the winner of the Kentucky Derby horse race is frequently the victor by a "nose"—a small margin measured by less than one step. Although the race is run over a great distance, the winner is not significantly faster than the second place horse... just marginally so. By doing many little things fractionally better than the other horses over a period of time, the victor wins the race. This is often the case in business. You do not have to be superior to the competition "by a mile." Just execute everything fractionally better, and the results multiply and place you in position to win. This can mean your decision to make one more sales call, dig one level deeper into data, or double check your cash drawer twice instead of once for accuracy. Apply this to your particular job, and see opportunities to differentiate yourself from the herd become evident.

Rarely are business results increased by large percentages from one measuring period to another. You rarely see twenty per cent increases in productivity or margin. On the contrary, gains are more frequently measured by basis point gains. That is, gains are usually measured in units of one one-hundredth of a percentage point. When basis point gains from multiple areas of improvement are added together, however, the result becomes significant.

Work-life balance

Organizations are quick to state that they encourage "work-life balance," but beware! This is cliché that may sound good on paper, but is rarely true in day-to-day application. They conduct annual employee surveys with results that frequently state that this item is one of the most important factors that relate to employee satisfaction. Post-survey, the organization's leadership makes sweeping statements about how attention must be paid to the promotion of work-life balance.

Within weeks, however, things tend to revert to the status quo due to pressures to meet goals and objectives.

Whenever possible, you must be aware of this type of behavior before you join an organization or transition jobs within the company for which you currently work. Work-life balance begins with you. It is an area that you need to exert some degree of control over. You can't abdicate responsibility for your quality of life to others.

I suggest you review the material in "Don't always say "Yes"" found in Chapter Three and review "Manage your manager" earlier in this chapter. These provide insight into the fact that there is no single solution for this situation. Instead, work-life balance is largely dependent upon your relationship with your management and others with whom you work with and for. You always have more control over the situation than you originally believed when you choose to get actively involved and not assume a victim's posture.

READINESS REVIEW

Your manager is a very important person in your life who has the potential to make the time you spend at work a rewarding experience, the exact opposite, or anything in between. Managers play such a large part in your career that your relationship with them can't be left to chance. It must be actively nurtured with a conscious plan put into place in order for you to maximize it with your Eyes Wide Open™.

The human emotions connected to the relationship you have with your manager are complex. You may ini-

tially be intimidated by them as they are an authority figure. They are the person in charge who represents the organization for which you work. Your supervisor is also the person responsible to quantify your contribution to the company, and, therefore, influential with respect to your continued employment. You may either dislike or like them personally due to reasons that have nothing to do with business. You may place them on a pedestal for various reasons. The net is that, if you work, you have a manager, and you have some type of relationship with that manager. Whatever form that relationship assumes, it is your responsibility to make it as productive as possible, no matter what its nature may be.

Make no assumptions about your manager's skill, character, or competency. Learn the content and substance of their agendas. Understand the goals related to their own career path. This is time well spent. Any effort you put against the discovery of what drives someone produces a deeper understanding of them. The mystery associated with why they act as they do is removed, and you become more able to productively interact with them.

PERSONAL DEVELOPMENT ACTIONS

- Review the last three one-on-one interactions you had with your manager. If you do not have such meetings, ask yourself why? When you do have them, do you get what you needed out of them? List three ways that you can prepare yourself for interactions with your manager in order to get what you need from these meetings.

- Remember when you brought a problem to your manager's attention. Did you clearly state the problem and its risks? Did you provide at least one potential solution, and perhaps two or three? When you next encounter an issue that needs management attention, ensure you offer at least one solid resolution, if not more.

- List the members of the Inner Circle of your immediate manager? Of that manager's manager? Do you either have access to or are you a part of your manager's Inner Circle? Know these answers so that you may leverage them in situations when their assistance could be valuable. How can you build bridges to Inner and Outer Circle members in a discreet manner? Knowledge of this beforehand can assist you when the need to leverage it arises.

- Perform an honest self-appraisal to determine if you are either consistently reactive or proactive. In which situations are you most proactive? Reactive? What three short term things can you do to increase the level of proactivity that will keep you ahead of the game? Write these down and refer to them often.

- Determine what your manager's goals are. When you are aware of these, you can more readily support them, provided they are reasonable. This permits you to become aligned with them, as appropriate. If the goals are not reasonable, you also know what not to support. Without knowledge, you are in the dark.

PART TWO

YOU CAN'T PLAY THE GAME IF YOU DON'T KNOW THE RULES

CHAPTER SIX
EMPLOYERS AS LIVING ORGANISMS

The first thing to establish before you decide where you want to go as you travel along your career path is to determine your current location. The ancient philosopher Lao-tzu, is popularly quoted as saying, "A journey of a thousand miles begins with a single step." Before you take that first step, you need to find out where you're presently situated. The material in this chapter directs you to confidently establish where you are today which provides a sense of self-assuredness as you embark upon your path. Get to know your surroundings and your immediate neighborhood. Don't be fooled with window dressing or superficial décor when you begin to examine your environment. In business, what looks like a palace on the outside can actually be a tenement behind the façade. The opposite is also true, so don't take this step lightly.

It makes no difference whether you are in transition from school to work, employed by a company, corporation, educational institution, or other entity such as a non-profit or even a government agency. This chapter encourages you to look around and observe your work environment with a critical eye. Give your employer a thorough review and examination. Lose your fear, self doubt, and any feelings of inadequacy you might have about this exercise. You <u>are</u> qualified at some level, and that level improves with practice and experience. Use the information provided in these pages to assist in the creation of an accurate picture of where you are today. Take note of who is in command, the culture they project, their skill level, leadership traits, and the other associated items that impact you and your life at work. You will be surprised by what you discover, and further surprised by how quickly your level of qualification to make these judgments increases.

Don't make assumptions based upon hearsay or reputation, but instead perform the due diligence necessary to uncover the information you need first hand. Trust only yourself and your own ability to make sound judgments. Don't be fooled by others' titles or personalities. Learn how to look pragmatically at situations and people, so you come away with factual information that is not colored by internal marketing, executive personality cults, cliques, or misleading data. Look for substance, and don't be surprised at how little or how much you might find in your research. I made too many assumptions early in my career, and almost without exception, those assumptions made me wish I'd done a more in depth, personal investigation into the matters at hand. It didn't take long to reverse those naïve decisions, but I found that when I initially based my actions on assumptions, the results were painful.

This chapter provides the insights that give you the ability to look at your employers in this new light, and as a result, be a more informed and properly armed person. While some organizations you encounter may be similar to the successful patriarch who takes care of and protects all the family members under his roof, others may be closer to the sick aunt who always is running off to the doctor to seek help for the latest malady, or even worse, the abusive parent who constantly berates their child and never provides the nurturing they need. There are companies that actually resemble the underachieving friend who is always an inch away from the next big thing, and even the quiet, nerdy cousin who spends all of his time hidden in his room at work with his technology toys. Whatever the case, you begin to see these organizations in a new light that gives you fresh insights.

Remember that you typically spend more time with your co-workers during the workweek than with your own family. This translates to the fact that your workplace is a very social institution that has far reaching impact on you and your team mates, colleagues, and co-workers. This also means that, similar to some family members, organizations may tend to act in certain ways that result in dysfunction or impairment either in pockets or over a widespread area. This means that your employer can be healthy or unhealthy, and not just relative to their financial performance. Include this possibility in your appraisal as you identify employers as distinct personalities, and you will no doubt begin to categorize them much the same as you might with certain personalities.

Much of the content in this chapter focuses on the identification of dysfunction and impairment within organizations. You must be able to recognize it, and understand its symptoms and root causes. This is a force that can be dealt with, provided your level of awareness is sufficient to permit an action plan that reduces and avoids its effects.

DRIVERS THAT PROMOTE DYSFUNCTION

No organization is immune

Every organization with a population of more than one displays some element of dysfunctional behavior at one time or another. None are immune. While some have a culture of either impairment or dysfunction across the entire organization, others have issues that are limited to divisions, departments, or other sub-groups. Which one do you work for?

Small organizations tend to be more intimate and personal with a culture that focuses on success for the common good, as well as support for their key individuals. An extreme example is Hewlett-Packard, which was launched by two men out of a garage. Chances are that the two inventors had squabbles that are typical of those found in ultra-small businesses. Just because only two people worked together, it did not mean there were no issues between them. Perhaps one slurped his coffee or the other didn't clean up his part of the work bench. The result in either case was friction between the two. The fact is that these underlying causes have the potential to produce disruption unless they are dealt with and addressed in order to not have a deleterious effect on the business. It is obvious from the results that Hewlett and Packard overcame whatever issues they had and launched a very successful enterprise. They were co-workers who built a vibrant small business that turned into a giant that still grows today.

Camaraderie across small organizations is at its greatest because the size of the group is limited and interpersonal interaction is high. Since everyone tends to know each other, every interaction has a face and a name associated with it. The employees' work is usually not anonymous. This tends to keep behaviors within the acceptable norm. One thing must be remembered about these organizations from an employee standpoint is that "small and intimate" with respect to the size of the organization does not equate to immunity from dysfunction or impaired behavior.

Large organizations simply expand the possibilities for behaviors that are counterproductive. More people, more personal agendas, more of everything means that the opportunities for an organization to display some sort of dysfunctional behavior grows with the size of the organization itself. In addition, the complexity of issues may also increase due to the same factors. Imagine Misters Hewlett and Packard have a dispute. They sit down face-to-face and discuss it. The issue is identified and it is dealt with in some fashion. Fast forward to today when the company has grown to tens of thousands of employees. Imagine the potential nature of those disputes. Imagine the possibilities.

The presence of impaired behavior in an organization does not have to be a permanent fixture. When identified and dealt with properly, it can be remedied and the resulting improvement may cause a reversal and a positive outcome. Individuals, groups, divisions, and even global enterprises may change their behaviors and increase their ability to properly function. Your key focus from a strictly personal point of view is to uncover the presence of issues and gauge your employer's ability and readiness to address them in order to effect change.

Dysfunction, by definition, is impaired, abnormal, and unhealthy behavior. Apply "impaired, abnormal and unhealthy" against your career or ability to make a living and you have the simple answer as to whether it is dangerous or not. It does not matter if this behavior occurs in pockets or is rampant in an organization. It ultimately has a deleterious effect on your career on many levels. It has been said that it is like poison ivy. First, you have to identify it. Then you try to avoid it but, if you can't, you have to deal with its effects.

Think about your personal situation. What is the one thing that happens repeatedly on the job that would make your life better if it was removed or fixed? This item may be a prime example of this type of behavior. So, this translates to the fact that a good place to begin when you observe a dysfunctional behavior is to ask, "What impact does this have on me?"

At its most extreme, dysfunction places your employer at risk and its viability in question when the root of the behavior is serious enough. On a more personal level, your role may come into question thus placing your job in jeopardy. The management structure under which you function may be compromised, and your ability to advance inhibited as a result. On one hand, it could be likened to a scraped knee that slows you down, but does not totally impede your forward progress. On the other, it could resemble a disease that attacks the body at every level with severe consequences if not dealt with appropriately. If you wonder why you wake up in the morning and you feel beaten down and don't want to go to work, you should determine if the dysfunction in your workplace is responsible for your personal state of mind as well as your compromised attitude toward your job.

The point is that this type of behavior in any form has negative effects. What is important is that you gain the knowledge necessary to protect yourself, and when possible, drive change that remedies the situation. While this may not always be realistic, it should always be considered, since an organization's future is the sum of its employees' contributions, including your own.

POWER POINT

CHOOSE PROACTIVITY

This has been mentioned in context throughout this book, but merits its own place because of its prime importance. There are two main methodologies related to how you address your work: reactive and proactive.

Reactive people take the victim's posture. They wait until something occurs and frequently react in ill conceived, poorly prepared ways that ultimately have less than desirable outcomes. Their success ratio in response to the issues they confront is minimal.

The second is to be proactive. This means you are aware of your environment and anticipate what may happen next. You position yourself so that you may influence the outcome of upcoming events, and ensure that you are prepared in advance when the inevitable happens.

The choice of whether to be either proactive or reactive in both your personal and business lives is a choice that you face today. This is not something that can be put off but must be addressed immediately, since it defines your approach to life.

If you are currently a reactor, strongly consider an immediate change in your behavior. Anticipate trouble and create contingencies for the unexpected. Ensure that you observe what happens around you, and seek ways in which you may act to properly position yourself before events actually occur. This minimizes negative effects and permits you to take the greatest advantage of a positive turn.

When culture degrades

Once vibrant, energetic companies can grow cold and lifeless due to the degradation of their cultures. Pure attention to profits, expense control, and finance-related line items diverts attention from the fact that an organization's people need nurturing and attention, just as the organization has a need for positive financial results. The ill effects of this are further accelerated by poor management practices that are often found in organizations with cultural challenges. The lack of attention to the human element that previously created a great place to work can have deleterious effects. Lack of attention to an organization's cultural health results in damage that is counterproductive to a successful future, since it occurs at the human level. This aspect of any business is the most difficult to keep well maintained and productive. It also requires the greatest amount of effort to repair once damaged. Think about it ... you oil and calibrate a machine and it runs smoothly. What does it take to keep employees highly productive and content?

Culture can rapidly change in even the largest companies. Sadly, based upon past observation, it degrades much faster than it can be healed. This is mainly due to the fact that the nature of many people is to become fixated on the negative rather than the positive. It has been said that a satisfied customer tells two to four people about a rewarding experience, but an unhappy individual shares their story with three times that many. This dynamic is similar to what happens within the employee population of an organization. A single individual may experience something that dissatisfies them and then share their ill feelings with their internal network. If there is sympathy for what happened to this person, the members of their network spread the negativity further. Others often come forward with similar issues that substantiate the initial complaint. This provides additional momentum to this groundswell of ill will. The resulting negative attitudes then give rise to cultural changes driven by the momentum of this negativity, which spreads with the force of a tsunami. Evidence of this may be seen in increased employee turnover or decreased productivity. In their early stages, these shifts may not be evident to the organization's leaders due to employee population size and possible geographic distribution. This hinders quick actions to reverse the effects of the changes and actually gives them a chance to become more entrenched.

It takes Herculean effort to maintain a pulse check on cultural health in far flung organizations. Even greater efforts are required to stem the tide once a shift in a negative direction becomes evident. Few employers of any size have this degree of insight into their employee base. Fewer have the designated resources at their disposal to maintain a pulse check that would determine these types of changes. Great organizations do not happen by accident. It takes investment and governance to stay abreast of the pulse of their employee base, and constant care and nurturing to thrive on anything but a short term basis.

Recognition of the fact that there is a problem may come too late to the leadership hierarchy. By the time they become aware of the problem, the well may be poisoned and the damage underway. Symptoms include employee morale that is on the decline, lack of motivation to excel, general malaise, and the worst case, customers who abandon the brand as they sense the negativity of those with whom they interact. People have choices with whom they select to buy from when they conduct business. Over time, they choose to spend their money where they receive value as well as a positive experience. The sure path to eventual failure is to ignore the importance of this experience. The absence of this basic success requirement eventually impacts productivity, sales, loyalty, and a host of other things that can cause the organization to unravel. The foundational issue is that respect of others, even at the company level, is a character trait—if you don't have it, it's difficult to obtain. It isn't something that is solved by the placement of a poster in the break room or the award of a plaque to someone once a quarter. Great companies have great cultures based upon respect. They truly believe in the values and do not just lip synch the words like a pop star diva.

Blind is the opposite of *Eyes Wide Open*™

We would prefer to believe that our organization's leaders are true stewards of everyone's best interests. Our preference would also be that they possess traits that enable them to execute their roles and deliver the most beneficial results for employees and customers alike. The truth, however, is that assumptions such as these place senior management on pedestals and assign super-human qualities to them when, in fact, they are as fallible as the rest of the working population.

Senior management and executives have the same frailties that haunt us all. They are not immune to temptation, poor decision making, ignorance, and all of the pitfalls of life. They have the capacity to drive an organization to become either successful or dysfunctional more efficiently and with more deleterious effect than any others in the chain of command. This is due to the fact that they exert greater influence because of the nature of their positions. Decisions made at the senior level affect an entire enterprise. They result in gains or problems of a widespread nature, while the average worker merely wrecks havoc in their general vicinity.

You need to know if the executives who steer your company are competent, adept, skilled, and experienced. If you feel this is a lot to ask of a team of leaders, you are correct. These traits should be the entry fee for qualification for the salaries and associated benefits that they are paid (notice, I did not say "earn"). These qualities are not common to all but a few members of the population.

As an inexperienced or new employee, you may believe you are not competent or experienced enough to make this judgment. On the contrary, it takes only a sense of inquisitiveness, common sense, and a pragmatic frame of mind to arrive at an accurate, albeit basic, perspective. Your initial evaluation does not have to be your final decision. Assessments may be re-visited and results altered as new information becomes available. The only imperative is that you view your management team through eyes that are not clouded by anything which might cause a distorted view of reality. Examples would be rumors, innuendo, outside forces, and the state of the economy.

Let's review several points that should be included in any evaluation. These are just a few that are intended to give you a start so you may gauge the competency of your own management team:

- Is your organization's focus on the provision of value for the customer, or is it more interested in the achievement of financial results? There has to be a balance here that is a winning situation for all parties. The greatest chance for success occurs when everybody wins.

- Does the executive team demonstrate a grasp of the details of the business as evidenced in the programs they initiate and the decisions they make? What are the last three major initiatives or decisions announced by your senior leadership team? Did they make sound business sense to you? Were they successful?

- Does the management team have a track record of success or failure? A web search can provide insight into past career performance of its individual members which may be enlightening.

If senior management in the majority of companies would be more honest in the appraisal of their own performance, our working world would be a better place. Misguided capital investment, lack of research & development, poor product decisions, needless wage disputes, unnecessary lawsuits, corporate lethargy, and unhappy customers are all barometers of bad management. This list is not all inclusive, but it paints the picture well enough to each other, but who possess little else to qualify them for the positions they hold.

Management's influence

The majority of damage on the job is done in one of two ways: first, through inappropriate action or second, by doing nothing when action is warranted. The critical decision that is not made when action is required is just as dangerous as the poorly crafted choice of action. When issues are evident and direction is needed, paralysis and inaction is not a solution, but rather the manifestation of dysfunction. Paralysis places the issue, and not those in charge of its solution, in control. Therefore, it is imperative that senior leaders seize the moment, seek good counsel, and make informed decisions which are the most beneficial for both their customers and their company. Only then can the negative effects of poor tops down leadership be avoided, and the potential of damage to the organization mitigated.

Bottoms up issues can occur and establish themselves within the lower echelons as well. These situations may hide from knowing eyes because the lower ranks are usually trusted to junior, less experienced managers who may not recognize or deal with these types of challenges. This kind of behavior in the junior ranks can be found in organizations where high level management acts in a similar manner. Senior management's lack of action to deal with problems sets up a bias toward inaction in the company's lower levels of management, which can facilitate severe grass roots issues. The situation may be further exacerbated when junior managers are not aware of the gravity of situation and choose to ignore it. Left alone, this state can become catastrophic to an organization, as it causes a negative, grass roots cultural change to occur that is very difficult to alter once it takes root. A prime example commonly witnessed is allowing employees to come in late, leave early, and take extended breaks and lunches. This permissiveness may begin with one individual, but can spread quickly to other areas if not rectified. This morphs into a cultural shift that spills over into other areas of the business, which causes additional problems. The snowball keeps rolling down the hill.

Since all eyes are typically focused on the top, it is not uncommon for bottoms up dysfunction to take hold and ultimately proliferate throughout the ranks. This is where it may have the most immediate effect on your day-to-day life. Recognition that this happens around you can provide an opportunity to take action related to the issue. Your awareness can be leveraged to address the issue, re-position yourself within the company, or look outside of your current employer to avoid this less than ideal environment, provided that it is severe enough to warrant such action.

Organizational Paralysis

Impaired organizations share many similarities. You only need to stop and observe the events that happen around you to see evidence of this. One common example is exemplified by the old cliché "Paralysis by Analysis."

In these situations, execution becomes secondary to the assurance that the plan is 100% correct and agreed to by an ever-expanding list of stakeholders. Trust in the individual contributor's competency diminishes, decisions by a committee become the norm, and the "everyone gets a vote" mentality becomes the rule. When trust in the ability of individuals in positions of responsibility to provide competent input to the strategic and tactical aspects of a project is replaced by decisions made by committees, it indicates that the company has lost its way. It is simply a vote of no confidence with respect to its staff. The damage creeps further into the organization as employees begin to feel a lack of empowerment when faced with decision making opportunities. A frequently seen driver of this behavior is management's lack of trust in their own ability to lead as evidenced by their reluctance to expose themselves as individual project owners. Instead, they hide behind the security of the committee and project a diluted brand of leadership that they hope may protect them, if the project does not perform to expectations.

A perfect example was found at a global technology company which launched a project to transform its tele- and web-based lead generation and sales capabilities. They were gauged to be five years behind their competitors in these areas, and leadership was tasked to catch up and leapfrog the competition. Nine months of intense focus on eleven individual work streams by a group of over forty subject matter experts was embarked upon at great expense. The group was sponsored by a Steering Committee that consisted of a division President, two EVPs, two SVPs and a COO. Therein was the problem. No single executive on the Steering Committee stepped up and actively led the project. No Steering Committee member became the voice of the working team. Rather, the Committee met every four to six weeks and offered cursory comments after they heard a never ending parade of staffers read slides that tracked work stream progress. In the end, much to its credit, the project delivered a comprehensive, strategic way forward with an embedded tactical execution plan to the Steering Committee. In response, however, the Committee did literally nothing to drive the work toward execution. There was no governance that enforced adherence to the suggested strategic plan. The same divisions of the company that were identified as the problems decided not to join the effort for improvement and suffered no consequences as a result. Six months after the team delivered its work, the project was viewed as a failure. In retrospect, execution was stifled throughout the organization by those who did not feel beholding to the Steering Committee's sponsorship. Neither the Committee nor any individual on it rose to the occasion and made the important decisions regarding governance and support for the work's implementation. When there was conflict between the deployment team and the groups that were affected by the team's work, the Steering Committee offered zero support. The Committee actually paralyzed the project's forward progress. They hid behind answers to requests of them by the work streams with comments such as, "You have to work it out." If a single Committee exec would have stepped up and taken a leadership position and demanded adherence to the agreed to plan, the outcome could have been that the work of the project team would have been implemented per the plan and the resulting benefits realized. Instead, the company continues to languish today and is once again launching still another project to overcome the same hurdles. Just as the last time the project was attempted, there is a Steering Committee in place, and governance is being avoided by leadership once again.

Also symptomatic of this behavior—and illustrated well in the example above—are projects that were previously planned and never executed that are then are re-cycled with little or no progress made toward execution. Lessons from the past are not leveraged, as previous work is disregarded and ignored. Progress is slow and the competition continues to move ahead due to this inability to act. Some attribute this to the lack of Knowledge Management systems within the organization, which could catalog and archive past work such as this for easy retrieval and re-use. More often, however, it is the result of executive leadership that has an insufficient connection to the operation of the business. They may have forgotten about past projects or believe that work on similar efforts is of no value and that the remedial project must begin totally anew for it to be a success. The past should always be reviewed before new work is embarked upon. It could save time and resources. It could indicate what NOT to do in the current work stream. Learn from the past to improve the future.

It is easy to make statements that call attention to issues that negatively impact business performance, but very difficult to make the changes to correct the problem—especially in the face of adversity. When a problem within an organization is initially recognized, several options arise. The first is to ignore the issue with the belief that it does no actual harm. This is obviously a bad idea, and the path that is usually chosen by someone who does not want to get involved for various reasons—none of them good. The second is to identify the harmful behavior, but then do nothing that remedies the situation. This is another poor idea, and one that is most often chosen by deficient people with few skills and weak spines. Another option is to both identify the issue and then actually do something to rectify it. This is the path true leaders choose to follow and one which is necessary to keep an organization healthy and in a state of continuous improvement.

Companies that have the misfortune to be staffed with leaders with weak or non-existent spines are doomed to mediocrity at best. It takes courage to "walk-the-walk" and be a true agent of change. Effective plans that drive change must include the re-direction of the efforts and actions of a broad range of staff members. It is not a solo effort. It also includes sufficient follow-up to ensure that momentum builds, and that the results will be successful. Walking-the-walk may be exemplified by the leader who understands what must be done, and then accepts accountability for the achievement of that objective. A perfect example of this was seen in an industrial instrument manufacturing company that had issues with opportunities that were stuck in their sales pipeline. These sales opportunities did not progress through to completed deals, nor were they deleted from the pipe after found to be dead ends. Senior management squabbled about who was responsible for "flushing the sales pipeline," but it took one enlightened mid-level, front line manager to step up and take accountability. He proposed a pilot project that required his team to not only work new leads but also nurture the stuck opportunities. The nurture process would either move the stuck opportunities forward or remove them as non-productive with proper documentation that stated the reasons why. The result of this person's eagerness to lead was a program that made other managers responsible to manage their teams properly. What a concept! Instead of permitting their individual sales agents define how they themselves would work the pipeline, the agents were given a pre-scribed methodology that, in the end, solved the issue. After the pilot was rolled out throughout the enterprise, the pipeline became more realistic and reflective of the true state of the business.

Lack of accountability

Does anyone get fired for failure anymore? Businesses' willing-ness to perpetuate the lack of accountability is similar to those days when everyone in elementary school got a blue ribbon at the science fair—even those who submitted inferior projects completed with Mom's help on the kitchen table the night before. In the effort to make someone not feel bad about his or her self, the playing field has been leveled to such a degree that, in many organizations, people are not held accountable for their work. Many companies unconsciously prac-tice what is called "the corporate shuffle," wherein incompetent or non-productive personnel are retained and not let go. They are either ignored and permitted to stay in place, or shifted from department to department. Both of these actions add to the dysfunctional state of the organization, much to its detriment. The reasons are many and range from fear of HR-based reprisals, lackadaisical record keeping, a poorly executed focus on results, and many others.

Whatever the reason, these businesses are reluctant to eliminate poor performers until the financials crash down around them, or a recession demands that overhead be stripped in order to survive. This practice leads to a decline in performance norms that eventually are felt by an increasingly disturbed customer base, which then leads to an entirely new set of issues that must be faced.

POWERPOINT

I SEE BAD PEOPLE

The spectrum of people you encounter in business is nothing more than a cross-section of society. There are quite a few bad people in business, just as there are bad people in every other aspect of society. You must protect yourself at work the same way you do when you are outside the office. You encounter quality individuals who are trustworthy, honest, and sincere, as well as those who are the exact opposite. Colleagues at work have been known to lie, cheat, steal, and much worse. Never believe that because you are in a work environment, that you are immune from meeting the worst that society has to offer. Never forget that the opposite is true as well.

Be wary of those with whom you work — and do not limit this to those with whom you have direct contact. Make a measured attempt to gather non-biased background on select co-workers as well as management at all levels. Avoid the rumor mill. Do not accept hearsay information about people, as it is usually incorrect, biased, and shows no respect. Do not stalk anyone—or appear to do so—while doing your research, but ensure that you gather appropriate background on this small universe of key individuals. It is simple to get the majority of the basic information on the internet on many significant individuals but, just as important, observation is a key to decision making about those with whom you work and work for.

Governance can't be avoided

Wouldn't the world be a better place if everyone did what was expected of them on the job and acted in accordance with the rules? If they did, we wouldn't need anyone to ensure that work was being done in harmony with established processes and the business plan—governance would not be required. However, since humans are human, the opposite is quite true.

Governance ensures that the guidelines, processes, deliverables, and their metrics related to specific operations within an enterprise are adhered to.

Governance is not easy. It is seldom a stand-alone job, but rather a function that is often assumed by someone in addition to their regular duties. It requires the assumption of the role of the moderator between the different stakeholders who own the individual parts of that which is being governed. It can be said that they are also the police who keep potential offenders in line while guidelines for behaviors and process are enforced.

Successful governance requires those at the senior level of management to take responsibility for the implementation of the programs and activities that they sponsor. This keeps them actively involved and provides support for the work in process. In smaller organizations, this is a simpler task, since the management and workers are in closer proximity, thus governance is more feasible and actionable. Geographically dispersed organizations find governance more difficult for the opposite reasons. That is why there is usually quite a bit of politicking involved to gain consensus before decisions can be implemented in dispersed organizations. In instances when consensus is not reached, certain stakeholders may not adopt the program or activity. This results in operations that are not uniform, which causes entities separated by geography and culture to conduct their businesses differently. This is known as a lack of syndication. It impedes progress toward consistency and efficient operation of the organization, and results in higher costs which impact margins. This makes governance extremely difficult to implement and is a major reason that it may become diluted or avoided entirely. The complexity becomes too much for someone to deal with as a sidelight to their normal activities, and nobody is disposed to commit to the task.

Think about how a fast food restaurant chain would operate and what type of customer experience they would deliver if they did not have governance of their menus in place. A burger in New York could be dramatically different than the same burger in Miami. The consumer would be confused and probably look elsewhere for lunch the next time they wanted a burger. The brand would be seen as inconsistent and the customer experience would suffer.

One thing to take away from this discussion is that a solution to an issue, situation, or problem without proper governance has less of a chance for success than one with it. All too often, organizations go to great lengths to define and deploy solutions to identified issues only to lack the backbone to implement the governing measures to support them. Some may feel as if governance is a dictatorial approach, but properly deployed, it is an inspection, measurement, and review discipline that ensures compliance within agreed upon guidelines that support longevity of the solution.

Clashing cultures and global dysfunction

If you work for a global entity, you should have a degree of awareness of how this affects how you. Small, local employers and multinational enterprises exhibit many differences, and if you are to take advantage of what is offered, you should know some of the differences.

Organizations with a global reach expose themselves to a greater set of opportunities for dysfunction than companies with a limited geographical presence. Time zones, cultural diversity, political differences, legal challenges, and local business pressures that clash with centralized global initiatives are just a few examples of these additional pressure points that can be counter-productive. Global entities must especially realize that these elements exist and deal with them in a manner that recognizes and respects differences, yet does what is right for the health and well-being of the organization.

Modern communications made distances become non-existent in the workplace. What happens in Germany is instantly known in Bangalore by virtue of our digital connectivity. An organization must, therefore, be cognizant of the impact that a local situation has on its dispersed population. Good news travels fast and bad news travels even faster.

It should also be mentioned that diversity and the issues it may spawn are not solely limited to global companies, since our workplaces are so much more multi-cultural than in the past. It is common today for people of different international origins to work side-by-side in local organizations. This means that sensitivity to cultural differences must be addressed and accounted for accordingly in order for the general organization to thrive at the employee level. Sensitivity, or lack of it, can result in either a workplace that is productive and harmonious, or it can be a caldron where issues simmer then explode with disastrous consequences. Your organization, whether global or local, must be cognizant about these facts, and not because they "have to." Rather, they should demonstrate sensitivity to cultural differences as this is the correct way to act and the right thing to do for its people.

Why do you care? The question has several answers: it is the right thing to do from a humanistic point of view; you more easily gather support when the value of diversity is recognized; different cultures tend to have slightly variant perspectives that you may be able to leverage to your advantage.

POWERPOINT

RESPECT

Respect human dignity—my long time, personal mantra—has never failed to provide a positive result. When applied across every aspect of life, second guesses about personal conduct disappear. Respect from others increases and you feel better about yourself. Your life is enriched through this is core practice that pays huge dividends in return, but never costs a single penny.

Opportunities for this approach are everywhere. The manager who does not make demands on her team that require sacrifice of their off duty hours shows her respect. A proactive offer to assist a teammate who experiences difficulty with a key task is another example. The simple gesture which permits someone to finish their sentence before you speak demonstrates your respect for their point of view. These are not complicated deeds. Many are done without the receipt of a "Thank you" in return, but that does not diminish their power. Start small and make this a habit that you practice until it becomes a natural part of who you are.

RECOGNIZE AND IDENTIFY IMPAIRED ORGANIZATIONS

Growing or dying

Two states of being exist in the business world: you are either growing or dying. There is no state of stasis. Recognize that your employer is either on one path or the other. Examine your employer with a pragmatic eye, since there are many variables to be reviewed in order to make an accurate assessment of your personal situation. For example, your company may have ended a steep growth period only to be caught in a downward spiral of events that threaten its future. Or, it may have ended the same steep growth period only to launch a new product that continues to propel it to even greater heights. Organizations just don't produce the same results quarter after quarter. The vagaries of their fortunes are not always evidenced by "steep growth" or "protracted contraction," but are often much more subtle.

While growth is the preferred state, it is not imperative that you work for a company on its way up. Business performance swings much as pendulums do—fortunes change from promising to challenging as they rise and fall over periods of time. Provided you are aware of the opportunities inherent in each condition, there are excellent possibilities for you in both. Businesses can grow, begin to die, and then be re-born only to falter once more. A prime example is the airline industry. They lose billions one year, only to recover and make billions the next, only to have the economy drive them back into the red yet again.

Businesses that are in expansion mode offer opportunities that have the ability to accelerate one's career in parallel with the organization's growth curve. Those that are on an inverse track can also offer good opportunities, provided management is aware of the current difficulties and takes steps to remedy the situation. It is imperative, therefore, that you do the homework necessary to make a determination of which type of organization employs you. This enables you to be aware of which way the pendulum is swinging and the opportunities that are available as a consequence. Remember: opportunities can be found in organizations whose fortunes are on the rise or in decline, so don't limit yourself and merely concentrate on those with only positive momentum.

Companies that are in distress need to employ specialists who are able to turn their fortunes toward the positive. Not everyone has this specific skill set, nor does everyone want to work for such an enterprise. Provided this is a skill that you possess, this type of company offers career opportunities that are not available in a thriving business. Therefore, it is to your advantage that you know who you are and what your skill set is, so you can properly position yourself no matter which type of company you work for. A select group of individuals have earned considerable notoriety and very comfortable livings from their successful turnaround efforts during their tenures at failing businesses. Success in this area of specialty can be both financially rewarding and professionally satisfying.

Another growth situation that provides above average opportunities is employment with a company that is fortunate to have the right product at the right time. When you work for an organization with a great product in the market at the right time, you are indeed in an opportune situation. Consider the early personal computer companies. They had row after row of inside sales agents answering the phones 24 x 7. These sales reps took inbound calls from people who had their credit cards in their hands and wanted to buy the latest and best computing technology. One such company, which has since ceased to exist, took over three thousand calls every business day for several years with an average twenty-two percent close ratio. They were fortunate to have had several great products in the market at the right time and at the right price. They did not, however, have the foresight to sustain that initial growth period through subsequent product launches and upgrades of equal or greater quality. They initially came to the market with a best-of-class product and a lot of luck, but luck is a fickle thing, and usually a very temporary condition.

Organizations with a leading edge product often find themselves in fast growth mode for a period of time until the competition catches up and introduces a superior offering to the marketplace. They typically have a technically savvy management team that lacks the business skills needed to grow the business efficiently. This is another situation where you need to assess your management team through a realistic lens. Even if you are new to business yourself, you must learn to appraise others' skills and their track record of decision making. Don't be intimidated because you're green. A good dose of common sense goes a long way to hone your ability to make good judgment calls. You get better over time. It doesn't take a trained nose to sniff out a spoiled fish. Apply this common sense as you perform a careful review of what management has done in the past to support the product portfolio through enlightened marketing and service. Also include what work is currently under way to develop the follow-on products needed to sustain the company after the current product's popularity begins to wane. During this assessment, you may find that your technically savvy management team's success has succeeded through dumb luck—that is, they brought a great product to market, and the success that followed was not due to marketing or sales expertise, but due to the product alone. This is often been called being in the right place at the right time.

Different organizations … similar issues?

Organizations follow patterns that match how they deal with the environment and business conditions in which they operate. The following examples illustrate how an organization's characteristics may create conditions in which less than optimum behaviors rise to the surface. These are common situations which can incubate impaired behaviors, although not all organizations that fall into these categories succumb and become dysfunctional.

The Fast Growth Company:

The Fast Growth business is in the right place at the right time with its product and/or service. This may be the result of the success of their market leading products that capture the imagination of their customers and drive explosive growth. Good examples are consumer or technology companies that enter the market with bleeding edge offerings that appeal to a broad section of people. In these cases, growth is primarily the byproduct of engineering or design excellence and not due to the competence or business skills of its leaders. This can lead to a great many errors in judgment that may impede growth or cause it to stop entirely.

Fast Growth companies are similar to some adolescents. They have the identical unbridled energy, and at times, the same marginal quality of judgment. They believe they are invincible, can't be hurt, and that their robust state of being will last forever. They assume everything they do is correct, because their current results are extremely positive. However, the reality is that many of these Fast Growth businesses are not able to deal with the increasing dysfunction that is resident within their four walls, because they simply do not see it. They are too focused on the construction of their immediate future, and not the improvement of that which will sustain them after the current rush of success passes. Their focus is almost always short term and centered on how to fuel the growth engine. Usually the responsibility for this growth falls to engineering, product development, sales, and marketing. These organizations may simply be myopic and not able to look at anything with the exception of a limited field of vision, which does not include the problems associated with the expansion and sustainability of the business.

When you work for a growth company, as evidenced by its accelerating double digit expansion in its last four to six quarters, you need to determine what drives these positive results. Become conversant with your organization's sales and expense data, at a minimum. You can find this type of information online in recent public financial 10Q statements, if your employer is a public company. A simple Google search provides links to this data. If it is another class of organization, you have to find supporting financial data that builds a case. Quarterly sales figures, shipping volumes, rate of new hires, and other pieces of information permit you to paint the picture. You want to look for double digit growth in sales in both yearly and quarterly reporting periods. You prefer to see operating expenses that hold steady or decrease. You should explore expense-to-revenue ratios to make sure they are in line with the industry for which you work. There are countless books on how to measure the fiscal health of an organization if you need education regarding what these or similar financial reporting items represent or where to find them.

Once you have done your homework and are satisfied with the data, ask yourself if you believe your employer has the right team in place with the correct skills and expertise to manage it to its fullest potential. How do you do this, you might ask? There is no trick or sleight of hand here. You just need to know where to dig and what to look for. Review the decisions that your management team has made recently. Are they sound and make sense from a business perspective, or do they appear to be decisions made without proper regard to their consequences? You don't have to be a Harvard MBA to review a set of decisions to determine the amount of intelligence, skill, and expertise that went into them. For your sake, the answer should be a resounding sigh of relief that your management team is a match for the job at hand.

A company with superior products and market timing has no limitations when the correct leaders are in place to leverage these conditions. Customer focus is a priority, since enlightened managers realize this is a foundational item in any successful enterprise. Obstacles are overcome in a programmed way without crippling the enterprise with debt, uncontrolled hiring, and poor investments. Extraordinary growth companies also possess an awareness of their future needs, and a plan for the achievement of longer term growth objectives. Long term investment takes an extended period to pay off, so its resulting burden may be construed to be a drag on this quarter's earnings by some who are limited by short-sighted thinking. Exceptional leaders are aware of this and know how to sell the benefits of long term investment and include them into the strategic business plan. This type of attention to an organization's health takes skill and expertise if it is to be executed properly. These attributes are resident in only a limited set of leaders, but when an organization is fortunate to have these individuals on staff, your chances for a better tomorrow are enhanced.

The Shrinking or Declining Organization:

Organizations have a life span much like plants and animals. Very few brands withstand the test of time. For every Ford or IBM, there are a dozen such as TWA, Wang Laboratories, and Montgomery Wards. Other entities, such as government agencies, Non-Profit Organizations (NPOs), and educational institutions, also come and go. Of course, there are some which seem to go on and on, but many reach a point of decline and imminent demise.

Their products or services may have not changed with the times or they may have been replaced by competitors' newer ideas or technology. For whatever reason, they are in a No Growth or Declining state and will soon need life support. Their employees must become extremely proactive and take appropriate actions in order to protect their self interests. This is the time to wake up and smell that cup of coffee that is simmering in front of you. Review the balance sheet, sales numbers, profit margins, and operating expenses. Dig into what is data available, and make sure you are informed with your *Eyes Wide Open*™. Responsibility for your own career must be put first, while you still contribute to the good of your employer. Place yourself on an aggressive path that ensures your continuity of employment. The fact that you recognize you work for such an organization is only your first step. Doing something with the information to sustain yourself is your next.

A prime example here is internet pioneer American Online (AOL). AOL once had 30 million subscribers and a market value of $220 billion. Its ubiquitous "You've got mail" alert for email was even the title of a Hollywood movie. Today, it is valued at just over $2 billion and has fewer than 4 million subscribers and falling. AOL Is a prime example that, as a company, you are either in growth or contraction mode. This correlates to the fact that your continued employment opportunities either expand or contract accordingly. History bears this out.

When a company has a leading edge position, it possesses a great deal of brand awareness that is worth huge sums of revenue provided that it is exploited properly with an eye on the customer. Wise organizations use this market capital to serve as launch pads for new products to keep their brand front and center in the customer's eye. Those who squander this unique opportunity typically do so because there is something seriously wrong in the Executive Boardroom—management has failed its employees and has placed the organization at risk. The result is decline.

Why this happens is not as important as your recognition that there is a problem afoot. You, as a proactive and aware employee, must have the presence of mind to recognize these events and take necessary steps to protect yourself. To play the role of victim as the ship sinks is not one in which you want to be cast, since it doesn't pay the mortgage and car payment. When you are caught unaware that there are threatening issues, it means you have been at work with your eyes closed and not wide open. Your goal is not to be a victim of someone else's poor management that results in your company's decline and possible extinction.

No longer the Leader of the Pack

Innovative products enjoy a limited half life of category leadership that usually produces an enviable revenue stream, dominant market share, and prestige. This, however, is a temporal state that any employee with their *Eyes Wide Open*™ should take note of very carefully. Innovation spawns organizations that may quickly rise to the top of their sector. While their meteoric rise is in progress, their competitors work diligently to copy, clone, and otherwise create products or services in order to participate in the gold rush initiated by the original. Imitation is a cornerstone of business, and no successful product lasts forever without clones that are designed to win at least a part of what the industry leader enjoys. While a net new product introduction is one way for a company to move forward, improvements to a competitive product offer a viable alternative, and one that should be expected by market leaders. After these competitive offerings come to market, the innovator competes with the clone's lower prices, additional features, wider availability, and other elements that tend to commoditize their original product. Commoditization of the once market-leading product soon becomes a reality, and the organization that once relied on it as its flagship has to take steps to remain relative and to maintain its leadership position. You only have to look at your television or mobile phone to see how pioneering products became as common as toasters.

These opportunities are either in the form of their own new product introduction or the improvement of competitive products currently in the marketplace. Since there is already a built-in demand for the existing product, the imitator gains an advantage through the insertion of itself into a ready-made situation. They do not have to establish the need for the product in the market, since the associated marketing expense was borne by the original innovator.

As an employee of either organization, there are both opportunities and pitfalls. Your opportunity largely depends upon how your employer reacts to the challenge it faces and whether it seizes the day or not. Knowledge of where your employer's products stand in the marketplace is paramount to your determination of the possible effects that this has on you. Are they market leaders or are they secondary, late to market copies? Do you work for an innovator or an imitator? Make a value judgment based upon what the market says about your organization. This can be found in trade publications, blogs, social media, and a wide variety of other sources. Track how your products sell and where they are in their life cycle. All products have a life cycle that runs from birth through death—often called "womb to tomb." Your recognition of where your company's products stand within this cycle provides one more point of information necessary to proactive career management.

Many businesses suffer dearly when their game changing product becomes the next toaster. This is the analogy that indicates that point where a product changes from being a unique, leading edge market leader to an everyday commodity. Does your management team have a plan that positions your product in order to sustain or gain market share, or is there no evident strategy? Be realistic here, since product position and opportunity usually go hand-in-hand.

Forward thinking companies' success plans are often found in the development area of the organization. This is where new products are born and innovations are spawned. A little investigation into this can pay dividends and allow you to have a look into the future. Companies for which I worked in the past often offered a product roadmap which outlined, in general terms, what was on the horizon. This was done to create excitement and to keep employees aware that they worked for a leader. Management wanted the employees know they had innovations in the pipeline that would maintain or accelerate their market position in the months and years ahead.

Organizations have two choices at the point of commoditization: either re-dedicate their resources and remain an innovator or relinquish their position and become part of the herd. While some companies have the skills, talent, and foresight to remain on top, others are "one hit wonders" that do not have the required follow-up product ready to be launched. This results in abdication of market leadership as the commoditization process rolls forward. This is not an "end of the world" scenario. Organizations that once led the way but became part of the pack still employ thousands who earn a good living and have perfectly acceptable career opportunities (witness Dell for PCs and Motorola for cell phones). The fact is that their employees no longer work for amazing growth organizations. They now operate within more constrained boundaries than the companies that replaced them.

If the challenge is not answered in a manner which addresses this issue appropriately, the organization and ultimately your job could become at risk. Growth fueled by the once primary product is now uncertain, and management must initiate the process to look for efficiencies that maintain financial results. The lifespan of a company's product may be extended through world class service offerings or successive upgraded versions of the original, but very few market leaders are able to sustain their ride on the wave of their original success. If you happen to be employed by one that has that ability, consider yourself fortunate.

Adverse to Change:

Some organizations handle change better than others. When they realize a new direction must be taken, they initiate a plan and execute accordingly. On the surface, this may appear to be a simple process, but there are many influencing factors that complicate change management. These make it an often tedious and politically supercharged undertaking.

Change can occur in processes, infrastructure, or with an organization's people. Change in any of these can cause discomfort, uncertainty, and frequently fear in the group that is affected. This can also spill over into the general population. You may notice change around you, and begin to think that you are next. This is natural, but it does not have to become a disruptive force provided it is addressed proactively by the employer. Look for crisp communication that alerts the population about what is coming, the timeline, groups that are affected, and anticipated results. This is the most effective route to minimize job paranoia. How a company handles this human side of the change process determines how much dysfunction is caused pursuant to the actions taken.

Change also happens with regularity when adjustments are made to the strategic or tactical execution plans in order to maintain the organization's health. It is critical to calm the population during these times in order to maintain stability. Nimble organizations see this need and act accordingly in order to address issues proactively. Directives are communicated with the resources affected, and the reasons shared in order to obtain their buy-in and understanding. Activities are initiated to put the change management process in motion, and the negative impact to the organization is minimized.

Other organizations analyze and agonize with no forward movement or momentum. The underlying cause of the need for change may deteriorate. The employee population notices the problems worsen and begin to wonder when its remedy will arrive. These stalemate situations are regularly caused by political infighting and turf protection that may cripple an organization and impact its performance. Polarization is a common side effect that frequently exacerbates the original damage. These organizations have a dim future, and should be placed on the watch list for possible loss of stability or worse.

Small and Understaffed:

There are organizations whose only shortfall is that they are too small and understaffed to handle the business challenges in front of them. Everyone does double or triple duty as the staff attempts to cover all the tasks necessary to survive. While this may be exciting and personally fulfilling, at some point additional headcount must be hired to meet the business's needs driven by growth. This takes investment and the ability to apply it wisely, so that the enterprise may ultimately benefit and generate a satisfactory return.

Some small business managers and owners may secure additional outside financing or invest more personal capital for the headcount. Others may ignore the need, and heap even more work on an already stressed staff. In any case, growth management is very difficult with constrained resources. It is further complicated when these business leaders do not have the acumen to manage an expanding enterprise.

This common small to medium business problem can be addressed in different ways, but it must be solved in order to keep the customer base happy and the business profitably in expansion mode. Many organizations fail under the weight of growth. A Las Vegas air conditioning installation and service company, for example, had three trucks and technicians, but too much business for them to handle with the current crew. The owner believed that if he threw more trucks and people at the work he would grow and prosper. He leased more equipment and hired more techs, but did not factor in the complexity of his new world. He did not consider the management challenges of a more intricate business model and the supervision of a workforce necessary to make it profitable. Dispatch, hiring, support, inventory, absences, additional tools, and equipment all made his business more complex than he could handle. He failed miserably in his expansion efforts, and eventually reverted to his original status as a single truck owner/operator. The downside of his regression was that he became saddled in debt and suffered a severe emotional setback. Frequently, organizations such as this have great upside potential, but they may also have a short half life and be out of existence when personnel issues are not handled appropriately.

It is imperative to know what type of leader is in command when you are in this type of situation. There are plenty of air conditioning installation and service companies in Las Vegas that grew and prospered. These companies figured out the methodology required for successful growth and executed to the benefit of all concerned.

<u>Grew Too Fast:</u>

This is another example of small to medium business hell. This type of company grows very fast which, in itself, is extremely positive. The downside is that staffing is not given proper attention and employees are brought on board who are not suited for the positions they hold. The result is dysfunction at multiple levels. Poor job performance, lack of productivity, poor quality work output, and customer dissatisfaction become common side effects.

A quarter billion dollar manufacturing company, which was in the middle of explosive growth, needed to address the customer service needs of their expanding client base. The decision was made to hire a Director of Customer Service to run this new department. The Vice President of Sales, who was in charge of the hire, wanted to fill the position quickly and get on to other duties. He extended an offer to a relative who was an elementary school teacher. He thought her caring demeanor that was required in her teacher's role would transfer to the Customer Service role. She took the position and launched an eighteen month term of incompetence that was finally brought to an end when she was fired by the company President. She was replaced and the company decided to use a recruiter to find a Customer Service professional. Quite a bit of damage was done, but the new Director put the department on a path to recovery and health.

The hope here is that leadership recognizes the fact that mistakes are made, and that they take steps to remedy the situation as soon as possible. If not, the poor hires become institutionalized, and the collateral damage continues long term.

Locked In a Death Spiral:

Your employer has lost money in successive quarters. Its products don't exactly fly off the shelf anymore. Margins are in freefall. Cash flow tightens. The first employee reductions have occurred. Morale plummets. Cutbacks to services result in customer flight to competitors. In a panic, the company looks for a fix, but just appears to make bad decision after bad decision. Nothing seems to work to stop the cascade of negative news you hear internally and in the media.

This is the Death Spiral. When a company exhibits these traits and loses its way, it is on the slippery slope to non-existence, or at a minimum, a vastly altered state of being.

Once in the Death Spiral, it is difficult to pull out and return to a normal, productive state again. In many cases, new management comes in, cleans house, and attempts to right the ship. Chapter 11 bankruptcy may be chosen as a way to re-organize. As a result of this, the company may be sold either whole or in pieces. Recent examples of very recognizable brands that traveled this route are Chrysler, General Motors, and Kmart. Companies that have ceased to exist as a result of their personal version of the Death Spiral are Gateway Computers, Lehman Brothers, and Enron. These were large companies, but this condition is not limited to the mega-brands. All too often, this happens to smaller entities, including mom and pop shops.

The Death Spiral is perhaps the most devastating and overt example of the effects of dysfunction. Very few fully recover. It occurs when an organization simply ceases to function in a manner which allows it to remain viable. Bad decisions, poor spending habits, shoddy products, and a litany of other examples may combine to bring down an entire organization and force it out of existence.

The ill effects of the Death Spiral do not end with what happens within its four walls, but extends into the community as well. Suppliers, vendors, local restaurants, dry cleaners, and real estate prices are all hit hard by this tidal wave of fiscal misery. When a significant employer shutters its doors, it takes a lot of other businesses out with it. This is even more pronounced in smaller communities, where small businesses have grown up to support the needs of the affected employees of the core, major employer.

The message here is, "Continuously pay attention to your organization's performance." Look around at what your co-workers do and how they act. Gauge attitudes about management, customers, products, services, and opportunities. Are real problems being solved? Is long term sustainability discussed? Look for passion or the lack of it in how co-workers execute their jobs. The lack of passion is a bell weather sign of future distress. You don't have to be a psychology expert to understand how behaviors translate to attitude and attitude to productivity.

Companies that are challenged exhibit negative aspects in many areas at one time or another. Trouble is initially evident in the executive as well as the general management ranks, since they are closest to the facts about the organization's health. An accurate early warning sign of trouble occurs when executives know there is disaster ahead, and begin to sell their stock or voluntarily leave for "other opportunities." Others pick up on the negative energy, and the quantity and quality of their work is affected. These key departures should be an early warning sign that something is amiss.

The object lesson is to run away as far, as fast, and as early as possible after the symptoms are observed. The extreme reaction here is that you may even want to physically re-locate to another locale with another employer, since the snowball of financial ruin could bring your community to its knees. As one national recruiter once said, "You don't want to be associated with a sinking ship if it can be avoided. When you stay too long, you are considered part of the problem that brought it down."

Organizational challenges

Small organizations exhibit many traits that their larger counterparts don't and vice versa, due solely to their difference in size. Some of these traits are positive while others are negative, but they eventually become a factor related to their ability to prosper and scale. These traits affect today's performance as well as plans for tomorrow's operations. They are the organizational challenges that must be met head-on in order to maintain the health of the enterprise and avoid a disruptive state. Your understanding of these better prepares you from both an offensive and defensive position relative to your job.

In smaller enterprises, these traits may include, for example, quirks of an owner, general management inexperience, questionable employee competence, minimal customer service capabilities, and lack of process documentation of key functions. It often also includes key tasks that are inadequately executed by less than skilled individuals who perform double duty (working two jobs at once) due to company size and a dearth of trained personnel. The business just can't afford to hire enough people to do everything that is needed, so the tasks that go begging are divided among its current staff. The result of any of these examples is typically less than optimal. Problems surface that affect both the company and its customers. The best of the best learn to deal with these challenges while others encounter difficulties that impede success with often disastrous results.

Larger organizations simply have more opportunities for dysfunction due to the fact that they have bigger populations, more diversity, and are more complex with respect to the number of functions they perform. The probability of finding work issues in a pool of fifty thousand employees is obviously much more likely than in a pool of fifty. As organizations grow, they change and become complex. Cross functional, interdepartmental relationships become more involved, and additional personalities are thrown into the mix. The chance for mistakes increases when more ingredients are added to a recipe.

Another group that has unique challenges is those that are in transition from either small to medium or medium to large. These growing organizations are unique in that they must leave many of their previous methodologies behind, since they are in expansion mode. This often requires that they adopt new ways to function in order to meet new business demands. They lose their intimacy, and almost without fail, begin to build walls and silos that isolate groups that were once cooperative, and whose efforts were formerly transparent to each other. Specialization becomes more common as the enterprise expands. Specialists by nature concentrate on a narrow field of focus and typically see less of the forest as they focus on individual trees. This leads to reduced communication with colleagues outside of their field of specialty. This alone signals the onset of wall construction.

Few companies of any size successfully prevent the construction of walls and find it extremely difficult to deal with their negative effects. Nearly everyone recognizes the symptoms, but few are able to cope with them. This is mainly because the departments in question are internally focused on their own deliverables that must be completed in order to meet their deadlines and objectives. These departments see their interaction with others to be of secondary importance. This is further exacerbated by the fact that they are often measured either by what they produce or how they perform internally ... not how their contribution helps the organization. Very few organizations have the clarity to measure teams cross functionally or as part of an entire end-to-end system. Without systemic accountability and a share of responsibility for the organization's total output as the norm, isolation is tacitly encouraged and dysfunction flourishes.

Culture

In addition to walls and silos, there are other influencing factors which may contribute to how an organization behaves, and what role that behavior plays in its success. Culture is another that is expressed consciously and unconsciously by the collective management and employee population.

Organizational culture is traditionally driven from the top down and then through the management layers and finally into the general employee population. An organization may have a published statement of values, vision, and their mission, which is intended to provide direction for how its employee base should act. These would comprise the official doctrine that is the touchstone for the workforce in a perfect world. The senior leadership's traits, behaviors, and decisions, however, create a culture within their tier of management that can be either the same or different than the organization's. In instances where the leadership is enlightened, both the real and the official cultural behaviors of the company are in synch. When, however, they are different, a very unhealthy situation develops, and the leadership is seen in a negative light as they act counter to the stated cultural norms. They are viewed as a group that says one thing and does another. Consistency always has a calming effect on the population, and cultural divergence works in direct opposition to consistency.

Even though cultural goals are outlined in a document or displayed on posters throughout the building, these things are meaningless unless the employer's hierarchy demonstrates adherence through their actions and deeds. The interactions between senior managers and their subordinates are the initial drivers of the manifestation of a company's culture. This is the beginning of the cascade effect. Every level of the organization looks to the level above and observes how they conduct themselves. When that level is consistent with company values and mission, that organization has a culture that is aligned with its published position. In cases when the level above acts in a contrary manner, the company exposes itself to negative attitudes and behaviors, since the employees see that the values are not held in high regard. They also get the message that it is acceptable to disregard them and act as they see fit.

Wait for pain before solving problems

Organizations that demonstrate considerable success may ignore issues that can damage them, since they tend to pay more attention to the positive things that contribute to their success rather than to the negative. Growth and success are the great balm that masks issues that percolate below the surface. Problems may be glossed over or ignored until there is pain—sales drop, customer satisfaction plummets, market share erodes, or products become commoditized as their market edge disappears.

Signs of this behavior can be seen in examples such as: when an organization's smug attitude (typically highest in rapidly growing companies) lets great talent leave because they believe everyone wants to work "for" them (not with them!); when problems are ignored as inconsequential, since the company thrives in spite of them; when budget requests to remedy identified problems are refused and investment is only directed to growth initiatives. These are just a few of the symptoms that any employee can observe. Similar behaviors are seen during interactions with customer as well, as this type of attitude becomes impossible to contain within the four walls of the organization.

It often takes a down turn in a company's financial performance or a negative business cycle to inflict pain before problems are addressed, unless the issues are so blatant that they can't be ignored. That, sadly, may be too late since much of the damage is already inflicted, the problem institutionalized, and the organization desensitized to its negative effects. Another common deterrent to the effective solution of problems is to ignore the issue because of a perceived lack of funds to apply against the resolution. Re-allocation of budget and resources required for problem solving is never convenient. It is always easier to direct it to items which fuel growth. This can become an excuse not to act, but it should never be the reason. Furthermore, it is an erroneous assessment, since the solution requires a change in how the organization thinks and not just how it spends.

Insensitive senior leadership characteristically does not realize that organizational health is similar to our personal medical well being. Problems get worse and cause secondary infections when they are ignored. Attention must be paid to identified issues, and the sooner the better. The way in which organizations handle their issues is a good indicator of their general health, management competency, and ability to achieve long term viability. Look around once more and observe how various problems are addressed where you work. Don't be too quick to judge before you have all of the facts at hand, and you understand what you are looking at. Some fixes solve issues immediately while others take more extended periods of time. When your data is collected and analyzed, your conclusion should provide insight into your employer's cultural approach to obstacles, which is a good indicator of how they confront anything that is a threat to their health.

Where is the customer focus?

The loss of customer focus is a hallmark trait of many dysfunctional organizations. Attend their internal meetings and track the use of the word "customer." You rarely hear it uttered. The focus instead is how much top line or bottom line revenue they can extract from those to whom they sell their products or services. The talk is about "selling to" customers, rather than how customers "buy from" them. There is a huge difference between the two states of mind that each represents.

All too frequently, the customer is viewed as something from which money must be mined. They are seen as a disposable entity that has a need for a particular product. Once that need is fulfilled through a sale, they are ignored as the company moves on to its next mining target. This is, in itself, a very short sighted view of the world. It ignores several simple facts: the initial sale to a new customer is the most expensive, and subsequent sales to existing customers are less costly since the expense of the initial acquisition is already realized. Considerable attention should therefore be paid to existing customers and their next purchases, which convert them into repeat buyers. This minimizes the cost of sale of follow-on sales, since the cost of initial customer acquisition has already been paid. It also results in the participation in continuing income streams and a larger share of long term customers' wallets. This strategy encourages them to become better business partners over time. Customers who are treated as business partners are also less likely to treat you as a vending machine, and only interact with you when there is a need to make a purchase.

Allow good people to depart

A very wise CEO of a company that thrived during the Dot Com meltdown of 2001 said, "Good people leave a company for good reasons." He meant that the departure of top talent does not happen without a cause, and if you work in a company where good people begin to leave, it is imperative that you uncover why.

When you bring a picture of a Bell Curve to mind, note that there are very few superior units of what is being measured on the right side, and likewise, few inferior units on the left side of the curve. The middle of the curve is heavily populated with what is considered to be the norm: undistinguished, average members of the group that is measured by the curve. They are neither superior, nor are they inferior. They comprise the norm.

What this illustrates is that prime talent is always at a premium. Those on the right side of the Bell Curve represent the limited number of workers who can be classified as superior. There just are not that many great workers on any team at any one time. That is why organizations should do their best to retain the best. When they choose not to actively retain outstanding performers, this talent is certain to be recognized by others who seek first-class people, and are willing make the investment to attract, recruit, obtain, and retain them.

Does your current employer let good people go? Do their internal obstacles and issues actually chase talent out the door? Good talent needs to be rewarded and not chased away. Take an inventory of the last few key departures of which you are aware, and objectively categorize them to see if they ran out the door or were pushed. This should provide an anecdotal view of where your company stands on retention of key human assets.

Financial slaves

Be very skeptical of your organization when its leaders pronounce that every quarter is "the most important in the company's history."

This statement is a common tool that management erroneously believes pumps up the employees' morale and makes them strive to exceed their goals. It is really nothing more than a statement that means that the management team is driven by near term results and lacks commitment to its future health. Some quarters are truly more important than others, but not every single one is the most crucial. Repetition is the problem here, and when you hear it, it should sound the warning alarm loud and clear.

The CEO and CFO of a company where several close associates work used to stand before each of their quarterly all-hands company gatherings and enthusiastically fist pump while shouting how this quarter is the most important. It became such a given that the employees used to bet each other how long it would take to hear this at any of these meetings. They became caricatures of themselves. The truth behind their statements was the fact that both of them had hundreds of thousands of stock options whose values made them increasingly rich with each incremental rise in the stock price. In effect, they were cheering for their personal wealth to increase. The side effects of their focus on the current quarter was a lack of key hires which were needed to sustain quality and provide customer service, the degradation of a once top drawer IT department due to the elimination of key positions to save money, and changes to the sales compensation plan which demotivated the sales team and eventually impacted sales. In the end, these two made their fortunes and left the company crippled and unprepared for the future.

In publicly traded companies, the pressure is always present for quarterly results that increase when measured year-over-year and quarter-over-quarter. This drives stock prices and investor value—the higher the stock price, the greater the value of the company, and the happier shareholders tend to be. This may lead to decisions that are biased towards the short term and ignore longer term planning. This type of thinking has serious implications on the forward looking performance of the company. The result could be that the current quarter looks good on paper, while at the same time, the company erodes its future potential due to lack of advanced planning and commitment to provide the resources necessary to build a strong tomorrow.

In public companies, this is predominantly caused when senior management pays too much attention to the predictions of the financial analysts who monitor their stock. Financial results for specific periods of time are predicted by analysts ahead of a company's earnings release. The stock's value is largely influenced by whether the company achieves these results. This heavily influences decisions made by the executive team, since they have a duty to keep share prices healthy and protect shareholder interests. Because many of them own a considerable amount of these same shares or stock options, the interests they protect are frequently their own. Therein lays the hidden danger of the use of their position to manipulate company activities to their personal advantage. When the stock goes up, their options are transformed into gold mines. When the stock prices decline, their options lose value or become worthless. The negative fallout of this is a narrow minded focus on quarterly results at the cost of longer term investment in time, resources, and planning that continue to build the company's future.

In private companies, financial results hold equal importance but their impact is typically found more behind the scenes due to the private nature of the company's ownership. While privates are not immune to shortsightedness, they do not have to worry about shareholder value, but rather investor returns. Typically there are fewer investors than shareholders found in public companies. The impact to the business is a function of the investors' view of what they want to gain from their investment in the company. They may have a longer term expectation of their return on investment, or it could be similar to the public company perspective. In either case, it is wise to gauge and be aware of the attitude of your company's investor pool when you work for a private company.

This is done when you pay close attention to current programs or initiatives that are sponsored by senior level executives. These programs usually need approval from the Board or executive council, so this may be a good indication of the members' intent. Also, pay attention to where investment is being made. This exercise is similar the assembly of a jig saw puzzle. The disparate pieces make the most sense only when they are snapped together and viewed. Are needed infrastructure issues addressed? Are additional essential employees hired? You need to lend an educated eye to where investment is applied. When you work with your *Eyes Wide Open™*, you have a good idea of what is and is not a good investment. Do not underestimate your ability to make these value judgments.

Promote from the outside

This behavior drives more negative morale issues and employee dissatisfaction than most others in organizations which permit the overuse of this practice. When a company hires externally and ignores qualified, capable internal candidates, existing personnel lose faith in the career path process. This results in an immediate decrease in morale within the organization. The issue here is that most companies do not accept the fact that morale currently suffers, and work overtime to prop up the external candidate as the best choice. An organization's sense of denial regarding this type of hiring practice has serious repercussions. This sense of denial becomes the order of the day rather than any acknowledgement that the reliance on key external hires is an issue.

This is frequently seen and especially impactful when a senior external hire is made. The ill effects caused by the external hire are further exacerbated as this individual looks to their past associates and subsequently fills open positions from their personal network. This once again ignores internal employees. This includes a pool of those who know the business better, have earned the respect of their colleagues, and should be considered prime candidates for promotion. Instead, quite often they are ignored and passed over, since they are unknown to the new boss.

Morale worsens when key managers or executives decide to fill vacancies that are the result of promotions through the use of the buddy system. "Ride the horse that got you here" is a commonly used expression in these cases. When a position opens, the hiring manager remembers who supported them in the past, and gives their buddy-list first choice for the open position. These past contacts are known entities to the hiring manager. Their strengths and weaknesses from previous experience are familiar, and as such provide a comfort zone from which to make a choice. The company suffers, however, since the best overall candidate may not be given a chance to interview or otherwise be considered, because they are not part of the newly promoted individual's network.

This practice tends to deflate the morale of the existing employees and most likely causes a negative impact on productivity. A further downside is that the newly hired individual may never get the full support from the team that existed before they were brought into the new organization. This group is very slow to forget how they were passed over not once, but twice. This results in collateral damage to the department over which the new hire presides. The effectiveness of the new employee is reduced, and the investment that the organization made in the recruitment and hiring process is devalued.

Acknowledgement that this type of hiring results in difficulties is extremely important if these issues are to be avoided. The inclusion of appropriate internal and external candidates in the process is a proactive step that mitigates negativity. It creates good will among current employees that is not earned when the organization's choice is to go blindly ahead with their external-biased staffing plan.

A prime example of this is illustrated by the impact felt by a respected technology manufacturer that hired a key sales executive from its main competitor. This individual then proceeded to import four other colleagues into key roles from that same competitor after his "poaching" agreement ran its term. This hiring practice was responsible for a total collapse of morale in several areas of his new company, since competent candidates were not even given the opportunity to interview for the open positions. To exacerbate matters, the Human Resource department denied that this practice was condoned in a public town hall meeting before hundreds of employees. This made the HR team lose all credibility. This team of ex-competitor imports had impressive resumes, but they did not have the support of the rank and file staff members. They proceeded to perform poorly, which led to the department's re-organization soon thereafter. This team was disbanded as a result and reconfigured under a new leader of internal origin.

Dependence on outside experts

This practice surfaces when management does not believe their internal resources possess the appropriate knowledge, skills, and experience to do the job at hand. They believe that outside consultants have superior, more informed answers to pending business problems than internal employees can offer. While this may be true in certain cases, these highly compensated consultants many times offer solutions that are no better than what could be obtained internally if management had the good sense to listen to their own people. Ultimately, it is a vote of No Confidence to the employees that are in place.

The end result of many of these consulting engagements is the misapplication of large sums of valuable capital that should be spent on more productive pursuits, such as internal resources that would facilitate homegrown solutions to the problems. The negative effects caused by diminishing the value of the input of the current staff cascades throughout the organization. This results in the demotivation and alienation of capable internal resources, which is then followed by a reduction in their productivity and an increase in dissatisfaction. When capable internal talent is available, the importation of consultants could be the choice by a management team that is out of touch with the abilities of their internal resources. Their choice to leverage outside help is only correct when the required skills are not available internally.

The decision to hire consultants may be the result of a good sales job by the consulting firm's Business Development team. Another item to keep in mind is that consulting companies often make the sale with their "A" team, but execute the actual work with junior staff members, the "C" team. These inexperienced staffers are known to use templates from past engagements that permit them to appear more competent than they actually are. They are usually managed by a single, part time senior member who also manages the relationship with the customer.

The result is that the customer gets very little that is new or ground-breaking. Rather they receive a re-hash of what worked elsewhere in similar situations in the past. The guidance that is provided is often recycled and does little if anything to differentiate the paying customer from its peers. The consultant's junior team walks away with perhaps the greatest benefit, due to the experience they gained on the project. This is not a "win-win" situation, yet it is one that is repeated over and over.

Look around at your place of employment and determine if there are consultants on site who do work your internal colleagues could handle. While there is a place and a time for consultants to be leveraged in the business environment, their presence could be a warning sign that poor decision making and devaluation of the current internal team is the order of the day. It may also mean that past hiring practices were not in touch with the organization's needs. When these practices are in synch with the business's needs, consultants are not required. It is imperative that the proper balance of external and internal expertise and knowledge be maintained. When this happens, most of what consulting firms offer may be completed with current staff.

Consultants can play a very key role in the advancement of the objectives of an organization. They are not always superfluous. They do provide specialty services when none are available internally. They may also offer expert, short term staff augmentation. They are not a panacea and should not be utilized as such to the detriment of talent that is already on board.

WHAT IT MEANS TO YOU

The most dangerous organizations

Clearly, the organization with the most potential to be helpful or dangerous to you is your own employer. Not every employer is a threat to its employees. However, when the hair on the back of your neck begins to tingle when you think about work, it may well be that you are entering the danger zone. There is a very basic principle of business survival that you need to place in your tool kit: listen to your instincts. Earlier in this chapter, key points were discussed which provided clarity regarding how to enhance your sensitivity. Culture, organization types, management, hiring practices were all suggested as places to look in order to ensure your eyes are open and your mind is at work. Now is the time to put it all together and review the results of your observations in order to assess your current position.

Become a critical observer of your employer. Understand that your workplace is more than somewhere you go to earn a paycheck, or a stopping point on your career path. Assess how it rates against its competition. What is your employer's reputation with its customers? Get to know your own department intimately, and even drill down to your co-workers' behaviors in order to more clearly understand what you regularly deal with on the job. Become an expert in the environment in which you work. This does not mean that you casually share your observations with your co-workers. On the contrary, your ideas and observations are your own and are most advantageous when kept private. What you learn is not coffee break talk. It is serious and should be treated in kind. The more data you have at your disposal, the better able you are to determine if the organization that is the most – or least - dangerous to you is the one that last hired you.

Employees are the heartbeat of any organization. Products or services may resonate with the marketplace for a period of time and deliver positive financial results. It is, however, the employees who drive and sustain the organization's success. It is the employees who deliver new products, marketing, support, and the sales revenues that drive this good fortune. They hold key relationships with customers and suppliers. In the short term, a company may be successful in spite of any internal issues it may have, but eventually unrest and unhappiness that can be traced to elements of dysfunction create an environment of discontent. It begins to erode the success your employer previously enjoyed. Minimally, this happens in those areas of the organization that are most affected, but it has the potential to spread to other areas when not dealt with and the root cause resolved. Take this opportunity to imagine how much better your employer would function if the unhealthy behaviors you recognize today were remedied.

This is why it is so important for you to know for whom you work and what type of organization employs you. Knowledge provides the power to make informed decisions. It is a wise individual who gathers all of the data at their disposal and uses it to their best advantage. The days of blind acceptance of your circumstances, and the feeling of helplessness that goes along with this attitude, need to be put behind you. Instead, transition to a more self-aware frame of mind that is pragmatic and proactive. This approach actually makes you a more valuable employee as well.

POWERPOINT

THAT UNEASY FEELING

Feeling uneasy about things at work? Get used to it since it's normal. Work is not supposed to be a consistent and smooth environment. Expect that things are typically a bit unsettled as your organization makes changes meant to improve productivity and profitability. These actions may not always align with your vision of how life on the job should be, and as a result, cause stress in your life. This stress manifests itself as nervousness about whether or not your job may continue, or that your working conditions could change. It is good to recognize that your nervousness is a reaction to the events that swirl around you.

It's here that an action-based state of mind is beneficial. Use your sense of uneasiness as a warning sign that a deeper look into recent events is required. It could also mean that you may want to be on the lookout for the next opportunity that changes frequently uncover. Ensure that any course of action you take prevents you from being blindsided by an unforeseen event.

Impairment and danger

Companies may exhibit some degree of general success and still be impaired, either in whole or in part. This means that there may be pockets trouble within the organization while the organization, in general, functions at a relatively high level. Departmental impairment in otherwise healthy organizations can occur. When you work in one of these challenged departments, you may be negatively impacted while colleagues in other departments thrive. This is another reason to be aware of the big picture and not just your immediate vicinity.

Departmental dysfunction may be an ongoing issue, or it may be something that is in its incubation period. In any case, it is dangerous and can spread if not recognized, dealt with, and its perpetrators dealt with appropriately. It is your personal responsibility to determine if and to what degree this occurs in your immediate work space. Whenever possible you should be part of the solution and not the problem. Address the issue and make positive suggestions for remedies through the appropriate chain of command. If management turns a deaf ear to your constructive input, then you can surmise that danger lurks, and it is time to re-position yourself in a healthier environment. In situations where you choose to remain with your current employer, work through your Human Resources department to find alternative internal positions. This should always be considered a viable course of action. In smaller employers without HR departments, you should network, review the job board, and do what is appropriate to your circumstance.

Whatever the case, at some point you will be impacted by organizational dissonance. That is, on the job discord, discomfort, or disharmony. There is no way to avoid this. Know that it will happen and learn to deal with it.

On the contrary, a state of harmony between what is and what should be provides a more homogenous environment where alignment is the norm and everyone is in synch as they achieve great things.

Does dysfunctional mean failing?

Dysfunction does not automatically equal failure. It may, however, translate to a state wherein the organization is not as successful as it could be. When a company demonstrates impaired behaviors that impact its customers and general employee population, it means it is on a path to a diminished chance of long term sustainability. Unhappy customers and workers and their resulting discontent eventually overtakes temporary market forces that drive short term fiscal success. The negative results of this eventually impact both income and customer satisfaction, which further exacerbates the already deteriorating internal conditions that result from these behaviors.

Another limiting factor that does not have to equate to failure is that dysfunction could be limited to a department that does not have substantial impact to the rest of the organization. The issue in this situation is that it does have an impact on the people that it directly and indirectly influences, even if it's more general effect is limited. Their attitude could be negatively impacted, and their performance could become sub-par as a result. These same employees may simply choose to leave. This causes further issues associated with reduced employee retention rates, also known as "churn." High levels of churn mean supplementary investment is required to recruit, hire, and train. It also means that the job performance level of the new hire may not meet that of the departed employee for months. It can also have other consequences that are not as easily identified depending upon the role the individual plays and their level of skill in that role.

There are also factors which disguise potentially serious issues. A new product introduction, for example, could place a company in the position of a market leader, and temporarily reduce the effects of its problems. A vibrant economy could further mask the effects. Other ancillary factors can also influence short term results in a positive manner, while the problem festers underneath the surface. It is incumbent upon you to observe and then determine your employer's current state of affairs so you may view your employment prospects in the proper perspective.

Problems associated with any type of employer can be properly addressed or they can be ignored by management. When addressed, there are two routes that may be taken: the issues may be either permanently solved or temporarily patched. Management that understands the importance of the permanent resolution of disruptive issues proactively assigns necessary resources and time to get the job done. In cases when a problem is addressed and the outcome does not permanently resolve the issue, it may be classified as a stop-over solution—a band-aid. The fix eventually erodes and the original issue resurfaces. The investment of time and resources is wasted, as the problem needs solved once more. On the other hand, when the organization fails to recognize and deal with a significant issue all together, it could ultimately be the cause of its demise and the sign post that points to its final destination.

READINESS REVIEW

Everything in this chapter is designed to prompt you to think about employers, in general, and the possible effects they may have on you. Too often, individuals are taken advantage of because they do not survey the landscape around them. They take what is dished out and assume a victim-like posture. This shares many of the characteristics with those involved in an abusive relationship. Conversely, it is a pleasure to see many others who build solid careers because they take the time to think about what they are doing and with whom they are doing it. In almost every case, the difference between the two is their decision to pay attention to both the general items as well as the details of their working life. What they don't know, they actively seek to learn. Don't let yourself be caught in a state of complacency. Decide to take action today.

Now that you have better tools to understand employers, in general, and how they affect you, it's time to turn to your attention to whom you work for today. This prepares you to concentrate on those elements related to your personal development. You need to increase your value and ability to contribute in a methodical fashion, so that you move forward on your career path. It is not an option to leave this to chance. You encounter enough situations in your career where chance plays a large part. Your conscious preparation and resulting personal growth places you in the best position to either take advantage or avoid the downside of what those chances have to offer.

You may currently go to work and think about your job and not a great deal about the organization which employs you. This lack of information leaves a gaping hole in your preparedness. When you include information about your employer in your arsenal of data, you become more able to understand the big picture. Without it, you are in a situation similar to someone working a jig saw puzzle without all of the pieces.

PERSONAL DEVELOPMENT ACTIONS

- Classify your employer so that you may determine where they came from and where they are potentially headed. Is your company small and growing or large and monolithic ... or some other category listed in the chapter? Is the right management team in place to see it through the next transition or do they, in your estimation, not have the proper skills to see it through? Know whom you work for and make no assumptions about who has their hand on the tiller.

- Review the most recent departures at your employer. These should include everyone from executives to line level staff. Do people leave for better paying jobs or better positions? Do they leave because they are disgruntled or stifled? Make an evaluation as to why they left. Does the company chase away good talent or did they leave for valid reasons? People often leave even the best companies for better opportunities. The opposite is also true.

- List how the last five management positions were filled by your employer. This includes managers, directors, and executives. Were internal candidates given ample opportunities or were outside resources hired instead? What was the reaction of your colleagues to the new hires?

- Determine if your employer uses consultants to do specialty work. Is this a common occurrence or is the exception? Are consultants leveraged to do work that the regular staff could handle, if trusted to do so? Does the use of consultants affect morale?

- Evaluate how real problems are solved in your organization. List three pain points that were either solved or still linger. Were these addressed only when the pain they caused became unbearable or when they were originally identified? The best employers look to solve internal problems as quickly as they solve issues in the marketplace. They know the negative impact that unsolved issues can cause.

CHAPTER SEVEN
EMPLOYERS: THE GOOD, BAD, AND THE UGLY

You have a job. You want to do your best in order to keep your career headed in the right direction. You are aware that there are many challenges in front of you, but if you're similar to most of the people who surround you at work, you probably aren't quite sure what they are, what they look like, and from what direction they may come. If you're fortunate, you work for an employer who is respectful and is at the top of their game in their particular field. You're doubly fortunate when your organization has a talented management team with the vision and courage to lead their employees through good times and bad in the pursuit of reasonable goals and objectives. Chances are, though, you may not be employed by this ideal company, and so it is wise to know whom you work for.

Employment is not always about being aggressive and on the offensive in order to drive your career to new heights. On the contrary, it is often about being watchful with a proper focus on self-preservation. An extremely valuable tool that needs to be well understood and learned in the earliest possible stage of your career is the avoidance of trouble before it strikes. There are warning signs that can be recognized which help you avoid these events. Knowledge of what to look for provides your first advantage. A healthy amount of paranoia keeps you mentally prepared and on the lookout for potential issues. Once trouble is recognized, it must be dealt with in order to mitigate its negative effects. This is best accomplished through your proactivity. Practice until these qualities become second nature. This enables you to own the tools that are needed to remain on track with the minimum amount of personal disruption. The net is that, as you ascend your personal career ladder, ultimate success depends on becoming a regular and active participant in your own career development. This is not a passive undertaking. You are the owner.

Trouble always finds a way to enter your business life at some level. Much of it can be minimized, or avoided altogether, when you are prepared and armed with the proper knowledge and skills. Not every organization is broken or run by greedy robber barons and faux captains of industry. Some are led by talented, well-meaning individuals who have the common good of everyone in their chain of command in focus at all times. What we look to do in these pages is not condemn any employer, but rather to create a sense of awareness of the possibilities that employees may encounter when they show up for work at the beginning of their shift.

VIEW THROUGH A CLEAR LENS

Vision, Mission and Value statements

It is important to understand how organizations are structured and how the different levels interact with each other. One of the most basic ways to relate this in through an explanation of how Vision, Mission and Value Statements are created and acted upon.

Not all companies create documents that are titled exactly as Vision, Mission, or Value statements. They may be called by slightly different names, but the intent is the same and the content similar. Those organizations that do create them recognize the fact that Vision, Mission and Value statements provide guidelines that ensure standards for how their business is conducted. They are always made available for reference to the general population of employees, so that the organization can unify it activities under their umbrella. Actions identified as counter to these statements are then seen as the seeds of dysfunction, and appropriate steps taken to provide remedies.

The creation of Vision, Mission and Value statements is typically accomplished through periodic senior executive planning sessions. Attention to this detail is a sign that there is serious thought given to the guiding principles that govern activities of the organization's leaders and employees. The participation of senior leaders in this process is intended to gain their buy-in and secure their ownership of the content. This makes the resulting documents more meaningful when they are subsequently shared with the organization. This is often done in conjunction with the organization's strategic planning sessions for the upcoming fiscal year. Alignment to next year's strategic plan is thus assured and the opportunity to cascade these documents down through the organization is realized. An additional benefit is that this review is also a valuable checkpoint for new executives who may have come into the company since the last planning and review sessions.

The Vision statement paints a high level picture of what the organization wants to be in the future. How this is to be achieved becomes translated into a Mission Statement. This contains a precise sense of direction that outlines how to support achievement of the Vision. An organization's Value statement may also be published at this time. The Value Statement is an affirmation of what the organization collectively believes in and how it expects its employees to treat each other and its customers. It should be the moral compass for everyone, and a reminder that the organization recognizes the need to walk the high road in its dealings.

The planning process is facilitated through the application of business realities and objectives that relate to the achievement of the Mission Statement. This drives the content of the Strategic Approach (may be called by other names such as Corporate Strategy, Strategic Pillars, etc.) for the upcoming year. This Strategic Approach has a limited number of pillars or main points that become the focal point for all activities undertaken in the ensuing year.

In large organizations, there may be five to nine layers of management between the executive group that identifies the Strategic Approach and the front line managers in charge of its tactical execution. These layers are always organized with a hierarchy of responsibilities that cascade through the different layers of management. Chief Executive Officers, Presidents, or other titles of equivalent executives have a primary function to set the Vision that provides a target for the future. They are the top of the pyramid, and their Vision should set the tone for how the company functions in order to achieve the goals to which it aspires. They also lead the construction of the Mission Statement.

The next level of management—Presidents of business units, Executive Vice Presidents, or other similar titles depending on the organization type or size—set the course for how work relevant to the attainment of the Vision is to be organized. This is often captured, at least in part, within the company's Mission Statement. The Strategic Approach is typically set at this level. Each of the executives responsible for a particular business function or business unit own part of the Strategic Approach. They are empowered to set the strategy within their respective organizations. They are also assigned associated objectives against which they and their teams will be measured in the upcoming year.

Vice Presidents then set the Strategy for the areas which they command. Directors direct the effort to create the Tactical Plan which places the Strategy into action. They work with their managers to create an execution plan for each of its elements. Managers manage and execute the elements of the Tactical Plan for which they are in charge.

As we get closer to the resources who do the actual work, we arrive at the front line Manager level personnel. These individuals are tasked with the execution of specific elements contained within the Tactical Plan. These Managers are found in sales, marketing, finance, product, IT, and various operations throughout the organization. They manage the elements of their areas that are part of the execution of the tactics contained within the strategy, which supports the Mission Statement which supports the Vision. These are the individuals who are ultimately responsible to ensure the success of the cascade of responsibilities from Vision to Tactical Plan.

In smaller companies, the owner/leader/CEO/President may set the Strategy and delegate the creation of the Tactical Plan to the staff. In very small businesses, the owner may do it all, but the net requirement is still clear—any business needs a Vision for the future, a Mission that identifies what it is, and Values that define how it should act. This may be accomplished through either a formal or informal methodology. Employees need this guidance to know where they are going, how they will get there, and how they should act along the way. It builds a sense of common purpose, and unifies efforts toward a unified set of goals and objectives.

Organizational life cycle

At what stage of the organizational life cycle does your employer reside? What are the qualities of the leaders who sit in command? Do these leaders' skills match the requirements driven by the life cycle stage in which you operate? The answers to these are critical if you are to understand whether your company has the proper leadership to steer it through its current stage of operations.

Businesses go through stages of a life cycle. They may begin as entrepreneurial enterprises. If they survive this challenging period, they often experience a period of growth. Over time this growth continues and they become established and more secure in their market. They may then reach a mature stage where they the business is sustained for an extended time.

Provided that the enterprise is successful over time, it goes through all these stages. On the other hand, when it does not meet the challenges common to any particular stage, it may go out of existence and its brand disappears with it. In order to garner the maximum benefit to be extracted from any stage of the life cycle and to prepare the organization for ascension to the next, executives who possess particular skill sets that are relevant to a specific stage should lead the enterprise.

These are the stewards who recognize where a business is and where it is headed. They leverage this knowledge and use it to keep the enterprise healthy and nurture its growth.

On the other hand, leaders who do not have this insight and who are do not have "stage appropriate skills" may miss opportunities that those with a better skills match would realize and exploit. They may mis-manage or not take advantage of an edge that their organization could enjoy in the marketplace. This is why this point is so relevant. You need to know what stage your organization is in, what type of leadership you need, and what type you actually have.

In order to more fully understand the life cycle stages, the following examples are provided. Timeframes that define their movement from stage-to-stage of maturation are not offered, since the duration organizations spend in one stage or another is inconsistent. Whereas, we previously reviewed the state of health that different organizations may exhibit, the following categories address the factors which may influence how different organizations are categorized on their road to longevity.

There are no hard and fast rules that govern these categories. Even companies of the same size and industry vertical do not act alike. One is not better than the other. All offer opportunities for vibrant and fulfilling careers when you position yourself wisely and keep your *Eyes Wide Open™*.

Entrepreneurial:

Entrepreneurs—whether they have technical or non-technical backgrounds—are good at start up ventures due to their expertise in the product area, but often underperform when business growth must be managed. They are best at being entrepreneurs and their companies are typically entrepreneurial in nature. They often fall down as leaders of a growing organization, as this is not their core competency. They frequently lack the knowledge needed to run day-to-day operations that are outside of the product or technical areas. Budget management, accelerated staffing needs, marketing strategy, and related non-tech functions can seem foreign to them if their background is not business-based. The more intelligent, insightful members of this group reach out to employ business expertise in order to overcome their own deficiencies. Those who do not may have their companies thrive for a period then stall due to their undeveloped management practices, misguided decisions, and strategies that misfire as a result of their lack of knowledge in areas that are critical to the growth of a successful enterprise. The correct talent in the correct position must be the norm in this day and age of thin margins and intense competition.

The guidance of the maturation and growth of any enterprise is a skill that must include the attainment of increasing revenue targets while expenses remain under control. It is a delicate tightrope act that can prove fatal if the balance between cash flow and expense is not carefully orchestrated. This is a very specialized field and one in which there is not an abundance of talent. It's for this reason that very few successful companies have the same executives in place at the five year mark than they did at start up. There may be a couple who are still in residence, but the original team is often replaced by specialists, or they have chosen to leave with a generous parachute courtesy of the successful run up of profits and market value from the first few years of explosive growth.

One particularly relevant category which illustrates companies in this phase is technology. These are engineering or high tech organizations that, if in the early stage of their existence, may be explosive growth engines whose officers primarily have technology backgrounds. These may get off to a fast start, hockey stick type of growth pattern due to product superiority or innovation. Their leadership teams can be overwhelmed by the management demands of a growing company, since much of what they encounter is foreign to their technology experience and background. The first set of this type of organization's leaders is frequently more comfortable in the lab than in the Executive Boardroom. These can actually be great companies to work for when their management staffs know their limitations and are willing to import skilled and experienced individuals whose core competencies map to the situation at hand. These companies need to have leadership that has experience, skills, and knowledge that go beyond engineering, and include how to successfully grow and manage a business.

Growth:

Growth specialists are hired to sustain the continued success of an organization originally run by entrepreneurs. This occurs at the point in time where the original entrepreneurs realize their management limitations, or the technologists want to get back to the lab and develop another breakthrough product. Revenue growth is in double digit quarter-over-quarter growth, and the business requires that their executives spend more time on management and less time on their core interests. The secret for continued expansion is for the original executive team to recruit and secure the correct growth team, which includes those who have this unique skill. In cases where the right team is assembled and are provided the leverage to do what is necessary to continue the organization's good fortune, there is a good chance of success. Growth specialists can also destroy a viable growth enterprise when they are not a match for the task at hand, or when they do not possess the documented track record and demonstrated skill needed to achieve success. An executive's resume may paint a beautiful picture, but the proof is in their actual history and performance—not in what they claim it to be. This is not an On the Job (OJT) training position.

Towards maturity:

The Growth executive team eventually needs to be replaced or augmented by one that manages the organization's sustained success as it moves toward maturity. Maturity is that stage where market share is established to the point where viability is not a question, but the amount of market share that can be gained is. Management of a more mature company is also a specialty. It is also one that requires a different skill set than management of an organization that is in rapid growth mode. When organizations grow, their complexity expands as well. Systems, processes, finances, and general management associated with a more intricate enterprise become the norm. Smart management teams (and Boards of Directors, where applicable) recognize this and take proactive steps to ensure the proper leadership is in place to match the need. Your recognition of these facts gives you another place where you may get a pulse check on the health of your employer.

Mature:

These teams eventually need to be replaced by yet another type of executive skill set when the organization begins to stabilize and mature. This new group must be one that has demonstrated success in the management of sustained growth as well as the transition to stability and maturity in similar operations. These individuals should excel as the principal drivers of initiatives that turn the organization into a consistent market leader. As a company matures, it may often move into a more predictable, less volatile stage. Profits and losses are subject to fewer severe swings. Market position becomes more firmly entrenched, and brand familiarity becomes more ubiquitous. This stage of a company's life cycle requires cost control, continuous product investment, brand expansion, and a culture of sustained excellence across all departments. This is much different than either the entrepreneur or rapid growth skill set. It requires a balanced strategy to address the longer term view, and the management of short term results. It is not unusual for a management change at this point, wherein at least several key members are replaced with others who have backgrounds that are more in harmony with the mission at hand.

Remember that the management teams that run these different types of organizations are not summarily kicked out of the door and new blood inserted into the enterprise. The best executives have an idea of what management skills they possess and what roles they best execute. They also know what situations make them fulfilled and, therefore, look to leave companies when they see their current situation is no longer a match or appears to be headed in that direction. This organic shift in the leadership team usually provides opportunity for new resources to be brought on board who more accurately align with the organization's needs.

When this does not naturally occur, many organizations' Board of Directors (or their equivalents) take steps to make changes at the top. They replace those whose time has come and gone with new talent that is better suited to the current business environment. Those organizations that don't step up and make necessary change languish as senior leadership stays beyond their productive time, and the opportunity for optimization passes.

Summary

Leadership of a company at any stage of its existence is not something to be "learned while you earn." It isn't a place where people come to be trained on how to succeed. This is a time to have proven winners in place who have a track record of excellence in similar positions. You need to connect the dots between who is in place today, and if they are the correct person for the role they play.

Evidence of the importance of these hires at the highest level is evidenced by analysis in the media whenever a CEO of a corporation leaves or is replaced. There is always editorial commentary that explores whether or not they are a match to the job at hand, and if they have relative experience. Their backgrounds are explored. Their strengths and weaknesses diagnosed. You can't minimize their importance.

When a management change happens, you must be wary of how the business is steered through the transition stage. Be prepared to do what is in your best interest based on what you observe. You might choose to remain vigilant, stay with the company, and fully support the new team, or leave in an orderly and non-emotional manner. The latter should only be done if your lack of confidence in the new leadership's ability and skills is severe enough to move you toward a change of jobs in order to maintain your own career goals. Your reaction could also mean doing nothing drastic. Simply sit back and be confident that you are aware and prepared to act if action is necessary.

Signs of trouble brewing

Signs of trouble begin to show themselves when companies begin to unravel. They are impossible to hide. You do not have to look at the balance sheet to detect these, but just look at those who work around you and take note of their attitude toward their job and the organization, in general. Your co-workers can sense when something is amiss. They begin to adopt an attitude of cynicism, which is not present in healthy enterprises.

One indication that leadership has lost its connection with their employees occurs when they roll out an initiative which is met with skepticism and cynicism. Moans and groans can be heard from the employees before they even have a chance to fully digest the program. There could be varied reasons for them to have this attitude. A few examples are: previous failed projects, poor internal marketing, or program goals that do not offer a "win-win" for everyone. The reason is secondary to the fact that the proposed initiative has elicited a negative response from the rank and file.

Unless management acknowledges this is a reality and undertakes their own program to solve the root cause, this attitude could have both direct and side effects that imperil the organization. When leadership loses the support of the employees, morale suffers, productivity plunges, and the organization is effectively split into two parts—management vs. employees.

One of the most successful initiatives I saw in business occurred when a group of executives stood before the employees and stated that the management team was at fault for recent setbacks. They not only took the blame for their past poor decisions, but announced a program designed to resolve the problem. Updates were periodically provided along the way to the employees who slowly came around and began to support management once more. Morale improved, productivity increased, and discussions about leaving the company for other opportunities abated.

Negativity within the general employee population is exacerbated when the organization in question goes through a tough period. As a baseline, the employees are typically skeptical of the management team. Their trust in them is already on the wane. It's the blame game wherein they look for someone to point their finger at and hold accountable for the current state of affairs. Employees can sense when something is amiss. The worst thing management can do at this point is to assign blame to anything other than the true root cause of the problem. When they either try to deflect responsibility or show ignorance of the situation, they lose control. Employees can see through any double-speak management may use as they attempt to convince them that current problems are caused by something other than the truth. Employees are generally smarter than the organization's leaders give them credit to be. They also sniff out the truth when management makes misleading statements about upcoming changes, which are supposedly being put in place for the health of the company. Certain employees pick up on this, and their negative comments about management initiatives are heard and adopted by others in rapid succession. People tend to imitate behavior, when they believe that it is acceptable among their peers. Those who do not initially speak out do so when it becomes the norm. It is at this point where management loses control and their effectiveness diminishes in a downward spiral.

POWER POINT

DO NOT "EXPECT" BUT RATHER "PREFER"

This is a tactic that promotes sanity and happiness. Similar to many other observations in this book, it applies to both your professional and personal life. When you expect an event to turn out a particular way and your expectations are not met, you experience disappointment. When you prefer that the outcome will happen a certain way and it does not, then its negative impact is much less severe, and your level of disappointment is reduced significantly.

When you have a preference instead of an expectation, you become a person with a much better opportunity for happiness and contentment. Expectations set you up for disappointment, since they are often not met either in full or in part. When, however, you prefer an outcome and it doesn't deliver, the negativity attached to it has a much less severe impact. Thus, you more readily recover and move ahead. This perspective helps maintain a healthy state of mind, which permits a more wholesome approach to events, processes, projects, investments, plans, and similar situations. Take some time to review when you last expected a situation to produce a certain result and it didn't. What was your state of mind at that time? If you were emotionally invested to a lesser degree and preferred a particular outcome, would the impact have been less?

If your answer is "Yes" then you have a valid reason to make a change.

"Delusional" is not a management strategy

When management's dreams become their reality, beware. Dreaming is healthy as it creates vision, but in order for it to not to drift into dangerous territory, it must be connected to a business reality. Management teams must have a plan which defines actions related to the future direction of the organization. Simply stated, they should have a clear picture of how they want to guide the company in the direction they feel is most productive. Become familiar with their plan, and trust your instincts and experience to determine if it is healthy and productive. Their plans should be common knowledge among the workers and be crisply outlined with clear objectives. When this is not the case, then a situation may exist where a definite plan is not in place, and the organization is adrift in uncertain waters.

The second course of action that could derail an organization is the plan which is wrong for the time and situation. More than one company has been dismantled by an agenda that was not a match with the current business environment. One example may be a desire to expand into international markets while their domestic business struggles. How can the expenditure of resources and budget towards the expansion of a business in another country be justified when there are obvious issues to solve in your own back yard? A second common example can be found when a company acquires another business whose products are vastly different than their own. This is seen all too often, and the end result is that a high percentage of acquired business units eventually are sold off at a loss after they prove to be too cumbersome to manage and their integration into the acquiring company fails. There are too many other examples to list, but suffice it to say that all too frequently the strategic plan does not match business realities, and the results are catastrophic. Wishes do not make dreams come true. These results affect hundreds if not thousands of people with individual stories to tell—employees, shareholders, families, and sometimes entire communities.

While many leaders execute their positions with skill and vision, others become delusional with respect to their decision making abilities. Some believe that simply because they are executives that their decisions MUST be right, and that they MUST be deployed. Nothing is further from the truth. This is a basic character flaw and often showcases their ego-driven issues. Executives are fallible human beings. One only has to look at the landscape of failed companies and disgraced executives to determine the veracity of that statement. Enron, Lehman Brothers, General Motors and countless others serve as case studies for misguided leadership.

Egos are dangerous in business. They have the ability to cloud logical thinking and can cause the "Savior Effect" to manifest itself in those prone to this type of behavior. That is, the ego makes one believe they know all the answers—that they can walk on water—and that whatever they say should be taken as gospel. Success does this to many people and is a direct result of a flawed character that has enjoyed a period of success.

Merger or Acquisition hangover

Merger and Acquisition teams from the company that initiates a takeover may consider anyone at the acquired company as part of the problem and not part of the solution to the future structure of the organization. Their past contributions are overlooked, and their current status is not given the respect that was earned. Companies that are taken over can be seen as weak losers on the corporate battlefield. They may be generally treated as conquered nations. A few highly placed executives are typically well taken care of—at least in the short term—but the general employee population is seen as chattel that can be retained or disposed of as is deemed convenient.

You and your fellow employees may have built a solid business from scratch, but you could be perceived as knowing nothing compared to the takeover team—at least in their eyes. While this is not how they may consciously act during the post-takeover period, it is how many employees of companies that were acquired interpret their actions. This is one way to eliminate internal competition and establish a comfortable pecking order for the victor. There is a clear winner and loser mentality that is denied in the media and in those pompous speeches made by the new leadership team. In reality and with very few exceptions, those who were acquired lost the battle and are now second place finishers. The fact that you may have a superior solution or process in place means nothing. It frequently is either disregarded or replaced with only cursory review by your new master's team.

It is important to understand what your company's value was that made the purchaser pull the trigger and write the check. Was it the customer list, market share, technology, personnel, or some other valuable commodity? Your knowledge of this helps you place yourself in the most favorable position relative to your role, and enables you to take maximum advantage of the situation. Otherwise, you are at the whim of the incoming winners, and your future may be at risk.

"Best Practice" means Danger Ahead!

Contrary to what consultants and management want you to believe, Best Practices are usually a dream concept. A Best Practice is an ideal based upon how an internal process should work if it is optimized end-to-end and everyone adheres to the guidelines that govern it. Now that is quite a mouthful. How often does this actually happen in complex business situations today?

If an organization states that it wants to adopt Best Practices in your area, BEWARE. This is a common warning sign that Less Than Best Practices are probably in place. It is also an outright admission that it is not a thought leader, and that the practices employed today are not optimal, and may, in fact, not be functional.

Executives often direct their staffs to identify and install Best Practices for their areas, but is there a will and a way to make this happen? When an executive states that they want industry Best Practices installed, it actually means they believe their own business is not up to par. It is also possible that they may have "Competitor Envy," which translated means that they want to be more like their most successful competitor. They lack the savvy to know that what works best for one organization can't simply be bolted onto their own with a subsequent improvement in performance.

The pursuit of Best Practices is often a costly process that is consistently disruptive in the short term. Increased yields are only seen when true Best Practices are deployed by experienced staff members with sufficient governance to maintain adherence to the original design. This takes time, effort, and a very candid self-examination of what the new Best Practice is expected to replace and repair. The considerable effort associated with the research, funding, re-engineering, installation, and optimization of Best Practices can easily be underestimated. Furthermore, since their benefits are normally not realized until the next quarterly measurement period (or beyond), there is always the danger that their target installation date will be delayed and slip "to the right" as resources are assigned to meet the current quarter's goals. All of this is counter to what is required if projects, which are designed to install Best Practices, are to be successful. In the end, the installation process is a complex matter that in itself requires a Best Practice strategy to make the dream become a reality.

Consider that Company "A" sees a Best Practice in Company "B." They embark upon a project to install that same process in their ecosystem.

There are foundational issues with this line of thinking. Companies "A" and "B" may be in the same industry sector, but they are, after all, separate companies with different infrastructures. Company "A" simply can't reach into Company "B" and replicate something from a foreign environment, then install it in their ecosystem without all the variables taken into consideration. Unless they make necessary changes so the proposed practice relates specifically to their own needs, Company "A" may never realize the benefits they desire from the exercise. In the end, success is not a simple matter. You do not simply mimic what you believe the Best Practices of another organization may be, and install them in our own system. There are pitfalls which can, and often do, derail such an exercise.

An alternative that is often seen as a way to streamline the installation of Best Practices is to hire so called industry experts (consultants) to drive the implementation project. They may obtain benchmarks either from their own internal knowledge base or from a third party resource. They then do a gap analysis that defines what must be done in order to overcome deficiencies identified by their analysis. This spawns a project in their customer that is designed to install process improvements into the identified gaps. While this may work, it is an expensive alternative. There is cash outlay for the information, the research, and the implementation. Also to be considered is the possible business disruption, which frequently occurs when change is implemented. The end product of this work may be of sufficient quality, but there is always the question of how much has to be paid to receive the benefit.

A less expensive solution often overlooked by executives who are not in tune with their staffs is to leverage the talents, experience, and skills of their organization's current employee base. In my experience, internal staff members often have the capability to improve existing processes when trusted and given the opportunity. Since they are currently on the job, they possess a ground level perspective of the issue at hand that outsiders simply don't. I have seen mid-level staff members submit solutions to complex requirements with a degree of skill and competency equal to and greater than those produced by the leading brand name consulting firms for the same issues. Not once or twice, but multiple times in my career, internal talent provided best of class solutions equal to or superior to that offered by the most respected names in professional consulting. These internally produced results on par with what businesses paid hundreds of thousands of dollars for from global brand experts. In dialog with my network of business colleagues, I find that I am not alone in this observation.

POWERPOINT

CURRENT VS. FUTURE STATES

Whenever you are engaged in a company review, a project proposal, a problem solving exercise, brainstorming session, or in a review of your personal progress, think of the phrase "What is the Current State vs. the Future State?" This is a handy measuring device that can be used in a variety of ways.

Current State is how things are today. It represents the status quo related to what your measurements are with respect to financials, process, personnel, and supporting infrastructure. If, for example, your business has a ten page contract that must be reviewed by a customer before they execute a purchase from your internet site, this voluminous impediment is the Current State. It isn't the ideal, but it is what is in place today.

The Future State is the optimum design point for the future. It is what could be. The Future State of the ten page contract would be one page digital format document that the customer could easily review and accept electronically.

These two labels are handy when you prepare project work, since the Current State establishes the baseline metrics and foundation against which progress may be measured. The Future State then becomes the target against which work is directed. This provides the delta (gap) between the two, and enables completion of the gap analysis. It also outlines the subsequent scope of the work needed to bridge the two states.

Do you work in the Emergency Room?

Due to the intense nature of the pursuit of profit and revenue in business, a false sense of urgency often casts its shadow over everything that shows up on the radar as a project, action item, or a simple task on the To Do list. This creates a general atmosphere of helter skelter, instead of a calm, metered path towards the accomplishment of goals and objectives.

Everything can't be a top priority. One item on the Task List may be #1, but others must be # 2, #3, etc. There is simply not enough manpower, funding, and time in the day for everything to be worked on as if lives depended upon it. Unless you work in an Emergency Room or urgent care facility, nobody is dying at work! The last time I looked, there were no bleeding wounds to tend to, or severed arms to re-attach in the finance department, sales floor, or the server room. Everyone needs to take a deep breath and perform their jobs with a bit more serenity and objectivity.

In order to avoid this type of ER behavior at your own level, first create your personal priority list. What needs to get done with the utmost urgency and in what time frame? What are the dependencies for this to happen? Who absolutely needs to be involved and, more importantly, who should not be involved? What can wait?

The Emergency Room mentality causes poor decisions to be made, since they are arrived at in a rush and not in a logical manner. It causes additional expense, since things done in haste are seldom done properly and may need to be re-addressed a second time. Constant chaos also causes confidence in management to wane, since they are seen as the perpetrators of this behavior instead of being steady handed, even-tempered leaders who do not wilt under fire.

Dual reporting dilution

Some organizations can't seem to get their arms around the fact that dual reporting at the manager and above levels is actually an admission that leadership either can't or won't accept responsibility for this group's objectives. Dual reporting means that two masters are served who may often be located in separate parts of the business. An example of this may be a Director of Sales Operations who actually reports to the VP of Marketing and the VP of Sales. The perceived benefit is that both superiors in the chain of command get to share direction of the subordinate. This, however, is contrary to organizational design logic as well as human nature. It is a difficult proposition to have two masters, no matter what the original good intentions are.

Dual reporting dilutes the effectiveness of the individual by the fact that a lack of clear direction drives them to attempt to satisfy both bosses and balance the needs of each. This is a very daunting task, which leads to confusion at the position level and damage effective execution of their efforts. Another side effect is that both managers cause additional confusion through the promotion of their conflicting agendas. This leaves the subordinate in doubt as to whom they should support as they attempt to resolve divergent directions from their two bosses. In the simplest sense, who do you listen to?

The net result is that this style of organizational structure has basic functional issues that, if not recognized and addressed, eventually causes problems. Companies that do not realize that dual reporting is not optimal have severe internal flaws that you, as an employee, should recognize. When your employer engages in dual line reporting in your chain of command, do you know who is really provides direction and what your Key Performance Indicators are? If, for example, your manager reports to sales and operations, what tasks are a part of operations, and which are sales related? How do they communicate mixed goals and objectives downstream to their subordinates? Unless your direction is clear, you cannot be clear in your personal mission.

Employee Surveys: lots of talk, limited action

Employee Surveys are different things to different organizations. They can be a sure sign that the organization knows their current state of morale is less than ideal. Honest and nurturing companies use them as tools to identify pain points and to create action plans designed to resolve issues. Companies, whose leadership is less enlightened, use Employee Surveys as window dressing to disguise the fact that they really do not care, but must put up a facade to prop up flagging morale.

Review your last Employee Survey and take note of the change that it drove. If you noticed positive change, you are fortunate, since your company acts upon identified shortfalls. If, on the other hand, you noticed that issues were identified, but no actions designed to resolve them are in place or planned, then be alert as to the true nature of those in command. Change which results from Employee Surveys typically takes time, but the action plans should be public and timely. There should also be measurement of progress or the lack of it. Anything less is evidence that the Survey is nothing but a smoke and mirrors attempt to convince employees that management actually listens.

Surveys can be a powerful force to drive a company toward excellence. They are typically rolled out as a formal tool that employees confidentially complete in larger organizations. In smaller organizations, the Employee Survey may be a group meeting or a series of manager's meetings with results rolled up to an individual or committee. It is in your best interests to know what form the Employee Survey takes at your employer and how the results are acted upon.

READINESS REVIEW

All too often, people randomly wander through their careers without a succinct plan for their advancement from one rung of the ladder to another. Very few learn how to address the entire spectrum of variables related to their careers. In order to separate yourself from the herd, consciously broaden and deepen your knowledge base about every aspect of employment. This leads to a plan which then enables you to more firmly take your career reins into your hands and propel yourself ahead. One step, then another, followed by another.

In this chapter, you were prompted to examine employers and some of their characteristics. While there are no perfect employers that populate the landscape, you can make the most of whom you work for when you know more about them. Knowledge provides power to those who possess it. As you lift the veil and closely examine your employer, you come to more fully understand why they act as they do and why decisions are or are not made. This data provides context to your job and to opportunities or challenges that may wait on the horizon.

Employers are collections of people held together by ideologies, culture, processes, and a common need to succeed in order to survive. Your ability to divine how you relate to these and how you map to them determines your job related success, fulfillment, and happiness to a large degree.

PERSONAL DEVELOPMENT ACTIONS

- Classify the organization you work for today. What type is it and in which direction is it moving? Does this information appear to have an immediate or mid-term impact on your employment? If so, are there opportunities available that provide chances for advancement? Monitor the type, health, and direction of your organization as this may indicate what is in store for you in the future.

- Review the backgrounds of the managers and/or executives who run the organization for which you work. Are they experienced at steering an organization that is similar to the one they lead today or is this new territory for them? What is their track record of success or failure? Have their most recent decisions been in line for what you believe is best for the organization as seen from your perspective? Form an opinion so you maintain a watch, since their decisions impact your future.

- List three areas where, from your point of view, there is dysfunction at your current employer. How are these detrimental to the company's health and performance? Is something being done to address them? Do they affect you directly or indirectly? Proactive identification of dysfunction permits you to protect yourself and be less apt to be affected. It is easier to avoid the pothole in the road with your *Eyes Wide Open™*.

- Read your employer's Vision, Mission, and Value statements. If they don't exist, ask yourself why. These are typical tools that are used to focus the energies of an organization. Does your management team "walk the walk" when it comes to living the values contained in these? Who does and who doesn't? How does that affect culture and, consequently, how does this affect the integrity of the management team? Positive culture begins with leaders who live the statements contained in these documents.

- Define what "Best Practice" means to your employer. Is it a reference to an industry Best Practice? Does it refer to how well internal processes are optimized to get the most benefit from the least input? Is it an enviable look at a competitor who does something better than your employer currently does? While most companies attempt to get better in every way over time, this pursuit can become disruptive. Your knowledge of how your organization typically addresses improvement provides insights as to how you may productively join the activity or avoid unnecessary disruption.

CHAPTER EIGHT
SHOULD I STAY OR SHOULD I GO?

This question follows most of us throughout our careers. We are always receptive to a better work situation: more pay, greater opportunity, and a host of other career goals that are important to us. These often seem to be best achieved if we change jobs, but as one sage industry leader once said when he referred to job hopping, "The grass is not always greener. It's just a different shade of green."

There are many reasons to change jobs or employers, but it should only happen for good reason and always with a solid plan. The Department of Labor recently stated that most of us change employers ten to fourteen times in a career, so it is not an uncommon occurrence. This means that, when you are part of this group, you will get plenty of practice at this particular task in the years ahead. Make a conscious decision to get very good at it, since quite a bit rides upon your choices.

Neither family or friends, nor co-workers can make the decision to switch jobs for you. They may offer advice or make a recommendation, but this is about your life, not theirs. It is an absolutely personal choice that must be made by you alone, unless you are married or have a significant other. It is also a decision that must be made for the correct reasons. These are unique to every situation and individual. So, similar to your course of action to perform Root Cause Analysis, you have to dig below the surface to find out the cause and not accept the symptom as the driver.

When faced with a scenario in which a change in employment is a possibility, ensure that you perform the due diligence necessary to provide the greatest chance for success in your new role. There are many factors to weigh, and they all do not figure into your decision equally. Take steps to fully understand why this move is under consideration. Separate the subjective, emotional aspects from the objective, logical factors that influence your decision. There is no completely right or wrong answer here.

Recognize, analyze, and actualize

In today's world, work related life may seem to always be in flux. Your employer is either in expansion or contraction mode, and your opportunities subsequently tend to expand or contract in parallel. You like or dislike our job. New opportunities arise. Your career goals change. Many factors affect employment decisions, and as a result you periodically need to review whether or not the continuation of your relationship with your current employer remains in your best interest.

Job decisions should not be left to the vagaries of chance or whimsy, but instead must become a regular part of your work planning regimen. This should be a discipline you employ on a consistent basis, and one that ensures you have a defined plan and career goal in place at all times. Career paths are not to be embarked upon randomly, but should have a beginning, middle strategy, and an end game design. Along the way, there should be logical checkpoints that coincide with where your original plan dictated that you should be at that time. In addition, you must be able to determine your current location. It is a long and challenging trip for most of us, and it is imperative that you keep track of your progress much as you might track your progress on a cross country road trip.

Your decision related to whether to remain at your current job or voluntarily leave for another requires crisp and clear understanding of the motivating factors. If and when thoughts about a job change creep into your consciousness, recognize them as something that needs to be investigated. This way they do not become a personal and/or professional distraction. Left as an open question, they are a distraction that prohibits you from performing at the highest level in your current position. What are the factors that created this situation? It is helpful to make a list of pros and cons. The act of placing words on paper encourages the writer to think, organize, and examine. It also provides a documented frame of reference for a number of reasons. Furthermore, this should be a living list ... that is, its contents should change over time your situation changes.

It is imperative to know where to look for the drivers that are the impetus for your consideration of a job change. Is it the job, the company, the people with whom you work, the location, long commute time, inadequate pay, or issues with your manager? It may be any one or a combination of these or other factors. It could also be that a recruiter contacted you about a job with another company that piqued your interest. Whatever the reason, you must understand what is behind the fact that a job change is on the table. Also ensure that it is in line with your goals and or needs, and that change is made for the correct reasons.

Employ a methodology to balance these reasons between the need to change and the maintenance of your status quo. Begin by asking yourself some tough questions. You may be surprised at your answers.

- What are your expectations for improvement when you move to that new role? Do you expect your life to totally change? Do you believe that all of your problems will disappear? Perhaps these are unrealistic expectations. A preference for simple improvements instead of lofty gains is a much healthier perspective that reduces the pressure for success to occur.

- Is your move a gamble or a sure thing? Picture yourself six months into the job with all of the excitement of the initial change behind you. When your move is budget related, work it out on paper, but don't be overly optimistic with your financial projections. Remember, "things" have a way of just happening.

- Are you the cause of issues that make your current position untenable? It might be that you could be the cause of your own discontent. When you are serially unhappy with your jobs, it could be that the issue is you.

After you complete a self-investigation, the next step is to prioritize your answers, so that major influencers are separated from those which you consider to be minor.

Of course, the current state of the economy also needs to be taken into consideration when you perform this self check. Economic pressures on employers have an effect on your career and this factor must be taken into account any time a job change is considered. Other variables such as health, family status, and change of goals also impact career decisions. In addition, you may need to take strategic detours if the economy forces you to earn a paycheck in a job outside of your career path in order to meet your obligations and put food on the table.

This means that you should always be aware of the opportunities available to you to improve yourself and your career. Job hopping is not what is being discussed here, but rather the creation of a methodical, well thought out career plan that may include the departure from your current employer for another. Should I stay or should I go?

POWERPOINT

SET GOALS BUT DON'T BE GREEDY

It is vital to have goals that are attainable as well as ones that that encourage you to extend yourself, also known as "stretch goals." Goals provide targets to shoot at while you build your career. Reasonable goals are very important as they set the standards by which you measure success or its alternative. Stretch goals measure a more extreme measure of success. They provide a secondary target after you attain your base goal within a time period (I.E. your sales or quality goal for the month or quarter). They keep you focused and productive after your initial goal is achieved.

> Be successful. Enjoy the pursuit of your goals. The achievement of overwhelming success is not greed, but usually the result of hard work, flawless execution, and the combination of many things that come together at the right time.

Fight or flight?

Many people leave their jobs because they do not want to remain employed where they are and deal with various situations they consider untenable. These reasons can be anything that makes their current job appear unsatisfactory to them. At this point, they become faced with the question of whether to remain or depart. This is also known as "fight or flight?"

What can you actually change, and what is the potential cost to you if you choose to remain? What is your personal commitment when the choice is to stay and fight? These are two questions you must ask yourself as you evaluate your current employment. When you hold a position that enables you to work towards change on those elements of your job that are stressful, you may decide to remain and embark on a methodical change management project consistent with your level of authority, influence, and control. When, however, you believe that your role does not provide the level of empowerment required to facilitate change, you may want to initiate actions that ultimately lead to another position. Your third option is to remain on the job, do nothing, and hope for the best. This is a rather undesirable option with obvious consequences. You would probably not be reading this book if this is your choice of action.

A common malady of today's employee is that they see the company for which they work as being fraught with issues. Other employers appear to be far better by comparison when viewed from afar. While this may be true, the fact is that every company has issues. None is immune from the problems that are the byproduct of the integration of many different people from various age groups, cultures, education levels, and points of view into one place for a common purpose. No organization's practices are all Best Practices that work flawlessly and efficiently. None has the ultimate infrastructure that delivers needed services and capabilities to the employees on time and under budget on a consistent basis. The alternative to the current situation always seems better when viewed through the lens of discontent, but as was mentioned previously, the grass may just be a different shade of green. It is still grass. It is still green, and the issues that come along with it being grass must be dealt with accordingly. You must ask yourself. "Is the devil I know better than the one that I don't?"

Just because you are in disagreement with something at work it does not mean that you should leave the company or create a battle plan to overcome it. It is always best to invest the time and effort to come to a decision that places the importance of the issue in the proper perspective: should you or should you not take action and what should that action be? Some issues are simply a fact of life, and in cases when they are not of the type that cause too much disruption or damage to your mind or body, you may choose to ignore them. You need to judge the impact of the issue on yourself and, at times, others. You also must decide if you can influence change and decide if the outcome is worth the effort. Refer to other topics in this book such as "Conflict," "Control and influence," or "Agent of Change" for insights related to your situation. Pick your battles wisely and sleep on your decision so that you do not act impetuously.

Fight for change in the workplace can be a very stressful endeavor. It can take a toll on your health, reputation, psyche, workload, and other aspects of your time both on and off of the job. Weigh the potential impacts before you commit to a decision. The stress caused by your involvement in situations such as these follows you home. There is no possible way to leave them entirely at work. Always be prepared for this eventuality, because it is an absolute. You can't separate work and home when it comes to the carry over effect of disruptive issues.

Make a conscious decision after you evaluate all of the aspects of the issue. When that decision is made, put it into action. Think it through only once, but think it through thoroughly. Make a decision so that you don't second guess yourself.

If, while your plan of action is in execution mode, you find that conditions have changed and your original approach is no longer valid, do not feel bound by your first decision. Feel free to re-evaluate. Review the facts and update your strategy. This goes back to the previously discussed philosophy which states, "Make a decision—if it is not the correct decision, make another."

POWERPOINT

HAVE A CONTINGENCY PLAN

The course of events in our lives seldom takes the logical and expected path. This is why it is necessary to have a base plan in place as well as a contingency plan for when the base plan "blows up," and a change of course is required. Contingencies must become a foundational part of your planning. Always have an alternative to fall back on if the primary route becomes blocked. This ties in closely with your adoption of a proactive lifestyle and pays similar dividends.

Proactive contingency plans should be in place for almost every occurrence. The alternative is to be taken by surprise without a pre-planned course of action available. All of the facts may not be at our disposal, so "What if's" must be projected into our future. "What if" the company is sold to another? "What if" my department is downsized?

This does not mean to constantly worry to the point of paranoia, but it does mean to always be prepared to adroitly deal with surprises.

Run from vs. run to

When in the process of a job change, you need to ask if you are running <u>from</u> your old job or running <u>to</u> a new opportunity. This is a basic question that must be honestly answered, as it provides insight into the thought process that drives this decision. Additionally, it makes you examine your true feelings about your current employer. It is also a common question posed by experienced interviewers. Therefore, it is wise to consider this question so that you are prepared in advance to provide an intelligent answer in the event you are asked.

It is not a shameful act to run from a job. It is a statement of fact that means that your current employer and you are not a good match, and that you choose to remedy the situation through your initiative to find more suitable employment. There can be many reasons for this, but the net result is that you made a decision to leave your current employer. In this case, you must ready yourself to address this situation in any upcoming job interviews. Do not speak unkindly of your current employer or anyone at that organization. Position your reason for departure in the most positive light possible. Mention, for example, you want more responsibility or a better fit for your skill set. Stay away from statements that may make you appear bitter. Take the high road here once more, and make every attempt to remain positive.

It is always more preferable to run <u>to</u> a new job than to run <u>from</u> another. It means that you may have found a new position that appears to be more suitable to you for what can be any number of reasons. Pay, hours, working conditions, prestige, location, and promotion opportunities are but a few of the possible drivers that encourage you to run toward the new job. This should be evident in the enthusiasm that you demonstrate.

Is the cause of your discontent you or is it your employer? Can you truthfully answer this question? This may be difficult to answer unless you have the ability to be very honest with yourself. A truthful answer requires some root cause self-analysis in order to determine if it may be you instead of the company that is the cause of your discontent. There is no trick to this, but it does require an objective self-exam. This may cause a bit of discomfort, because it requires honest introspection. This question makes even the strongest among us occasionally wince with a bit of pain. It is a critical question to ask, however. When you move from job to job, never seem content, and always place blame on others or your employer, this question becomes especially poignant. It is similar to the story about the man who was married and divorced six times. He wondered why he could never meet a good woman.

When you find that the answer lies within you and not with your employer, you have some work to do. A positive point to make is that you now recognize you need to work on your attitude and to your approach to life on the job. This is a productive endeavor that, when done conscientiously, pays dividends well into the future. While it is difficult to strip away the veneer and look at the real you, the work is worthwhile and the outcome almost always enlightening. This is a territory where you can't be afraid to tread. The answers you discover drive your behaviors, and not always in a direction which is comfortable. On a more positive note, you may discover new and positive things about yourself that motivate you in ways that you could not have imagined.

The job search process

<u>When to look:</u> Look for a job when you have a job. This is a simple yet often misunderstood axiom. You should always be receptive to new opportunities for your next position no matter what your current employment status may be. This includes those periods during which you are gainfully employed. The world is filled with alternative opportunities that may be of interest to you, provided you remain open to them. This does not mean you should be engaged in an active, never-ending job search. It does mean, however, you should always be open to a suitable opportunity that may come your way. Unless you are an individual who is totally in your comfort zone, have a job that pays what you want, and a role that is in line with your skills and training, this means you should remain receptive to new prospects that may present themselves.

Openness to other employment opportunities provides the chance for personal introspection into a wide variety of areas. Personal preferences that are governed by your work (such as where you live, how far you commute) are also reviewed during the recruiting process. Remember that there are very few of us who spend our entire career with one employer doing one job. It is common for careers to include multiple phases with a variety of jobs in each phase. These phases may be in fields that can be different, but somehow aligned with the others, since what was learned in the past becomes a skill in the present.

You can be more selective in the choice of your next job when you are employed. Your current position provides a stream of income, and your resume does not have a blank spot that indicates a period of unemployment to a prospective employer. This gives you a sense of empowerment that results in an air of confidence during interviews. Unemployment often results in the inverse. Employment also eliminates many of the stress points that an unemployed job seeker faces. The unemployed may exhibit stress during interviews that can surface as desperation. This aura is transmitted to the hiring agent, who interprets it as a negative and may move on to the next candidate. The point to grasp here is to be open to positions that satisfy your desire for self-improvement during periods of employment, which is when you encounter your best chance for success.

Remember, though, that you do owe your current employer a day's work for a day's pay. Do not take advantage of them in any way that negatively impacts your performance or puts your credibility at risk. You must conduct yourself within ethical guidelines and remain productive. You may, however, take advantage of breaks, lunch hours, and scheduled time off to follow-up on opportunities that may arise.

Always be alert for opportunities. Network through associates, friends, and family, as well as remain open to calls from valid recruiters. Post your professional information on at least one job-related social networking site such as LinkedIn. These are searched by recruiters as resources for candidates. Be smart about your entries. Be truthful, do not exaggerate, and use appropriate descriptions of your background and strengths. Your current employer may review your postings on these sites, so be accurate as to your role and do not post anything that could derail your current job.

By products of a job search: Even though you may be happy with your current position, things change rapidly in business. You need to be prepared to seize opportunities when presented. Awareness of the job market allows you to hone your skills and focus development of those areas that are relevant to today's employment environment. You won't know what is relevant, unless you are in the market and not in the dark.

Passive job searches (your review of opportunities that may be either offered or discovered, but not an active pursuit of alternative employment) can actually assist in your personal development. You need to know what skills and competencies other companies seek in order to prepare yourself to take next steps in your career. Job searches provide this type of insight which can be leveraged in your current role. This can be done in a manner that is not disruptive to your current employment and respectful to your present employer.

Interviews for new jobs also are great tools to keep you current with what other companies are doing and how your current employer measures up against the competition. Since you typically interview for positions within your current industry, this information can become a valuable learning tool for you, even if a position is not offered. It provides insight into your industry that you often can't get within the four walls of your current employer. You should always be in information gathering mode during your career. The sum of your collected data permits you to not only contribute in the best possible way, but it gives you a broader and deeper understanding of your business.

Discussions with recruiters from outside of your company keep your interview skills sharp and provide insight into what is available in the field in which you work. They uncover those areas that need development, and highlight those areas that are your strengths. Interviews also force you to review your personal preferences that are impacted by a job change. Your response to recruiting opportunities forces you to take stock of where you are in your career, and to document what you have done to date. This can be very revealing as it may surprise you as to what you have accomplished in either the positive or negative sense. This provides a checkpoint against which you can plan further actions that are designed to enhance your career improvement opportunities.

Job interviews for which you are qualified are great ways to keep you sharp and on top of your game. Don't be afraid to do external interviews. Interviews force you to do an in depth review of your skills and competencies. They also require that you create and comfortably verbalize your personal "elevator speech." Your elevator speech is an approximately fifteen to thirty second oral statement of who you are and what you bring to the table professionally. It should also include thoughts that concern the various elements of your approach to work that provide insight into your values, career aspirations, and what you represent. Prepare your elevator speech before any interview to ensure inclusion of its salient points so that they offer maximum impact. Create it first in written form, rewrite it, and review it until one version stands out from the others. Focus on this draft until it becomes ingrained and natural in its delivery as it is spoken. This greatly assists in the creation of a positive impression. It also makes you more at ease, as it conveys key aspects of who you are and specific points you want to leave behind. Interviews are a good gauge of how well you present yourself. They also are a good measure of how well you are prepared to accept a new role with possibly greater responsibilities and rewards.

General preparation: Include a written list of possible questions you could be asked and answers to be offered in response in your preparation for interviews. This ensures that all relevant points are included when you answer those questions. In addition, most positions have Job Descriptions that are available prior to your interview. These list the competencies and experience that are requisite for consideration. Their review prior to an interview permits you to gauge yourself accordingly, and facilitate how you represent yourself in light of the position's requirements. Read them carefully and write how you match to each of the requirements so that you may visualize your replies during the course of your interview. This method permits you to offer smooth, well-paced answers that project your professionalism and prepared-ness. Also, make note of three to five questions to ask your interviewer. This is your chance to interview the interviewer about the company and gain valuable information that assists in your decision process. It demonstrates your interest and desire to find out more about this potential employer. Questions turn the interview into a dialog and not an inquisition.

Your resume and general cover letter template should always be kept current and ready to offer a prospective employer. This facilitates their quick customization, so that they are relevant to the position for which you apply. Another tool to have at the ready is a short one or two paragraph bio that provides a general recap of your background. These preparations ensure that you are ready to efficiently seize an opportunity when it occurs.

Continually improve these documents. Review and edit them repeatedly over time. Make corrections and edits each time you use them for your next opportunity. The internet has many sites where you may find templates or formats for these documents. Choose one that best projects the image you want to communicate. Next, compose mul-tiple drafts until you are comfortable with your current working prod-uct. Review your resume a week after you complete what you believe is a finished draft. In addition, have a trusted colleague or advisor pro-vide their comments back to you. A second set of eyes is always a good idea relative to any important communication. In both cases, you may find new areas for improvement and could find errors that were missed during the initial edits.

It is imperative that you use a personal physical address, email, and telephone number when you apply for work outside of your current employer. Not only is the use of most employers' assets a violation of company policy in most cases, but it is also just not smart. You do not want to be exposed within the context of your present job as someone who is engaged in a job search outside of the company. This could be detrimental to your current employment, and cause significant prob-lems if you are not offered the position for which you apply.

Cash smoothes out the bumps

Money provides leverage and options. In the context of your career, money in the bank gives you options to do what is in your best interests. A nest egg allows you to make choices that are not available without it. Financial planners recommend a six month cash cushion to get through trying times. This may be a difficult goal to achieve in many cases, due to the high cost of living and your general lifestyle choices. It should, however, be a goal that is taken seriously and prioritized near the top of your list.

Your cushion of cash has a secondary effect. Money also provides power and freedom. Since money in the bank provides a sense of security and peace of mind, it removes a major worry from your everyday thinking. This permits concentration on other things in a more focused manner and provides freedom from many negative aspects that tend to cloud your judgment. Cash on hand provides power through its ability to offer choices that are not available when you are cash poor.

You may have to adjust your spending or lifestyle in order to build a cash reserve, but the payoff is more than commensurate with the effort. It may also take a considerable amount of time to create an amount that can sustain you for three to six months. The alternative is to be one paycheck removed from poverty and emergency status. The lack of a nest egg places you in an economic state that reduces your ability to make employment choices, since you require continuous cash flow to stay afloat. This makes you dependent upon your current job to fulfill your basic needs.

Your cash cushion also provides you with choices that the lack of a nest egg strips away from you. You feel less tied to a job that is not satisfying or rewarding if you have cash on hand. Your savings also offer a sense of confidence that gives you the extra drive that only positive and secure individuals possess. Do not underestimate the value of this point. Consider the alternative, how it would negatively affect you, and then decide which path to take. In this sense, money gives you power to be more in control of your life.

Negotiations are hardball

There comes a time when compensation becomes the topic of conversation with a prospective employer. This is not an easy topic for most of us to address for many reasons that range from fear to lack of self-confidence. You may become extremely uncomfortable when you become engaged in a discussion about money and pay-based items. Whatever the underlying cause, the net is that there is discomfort which can lead to avoidance, or worse, a feeling of subservience. It is also common for compensation discussions to result in a fear that these talks may result in negative consequences and reflect badly because you may appear aggressive or self-serving. Some job seekers, for example, just want the position no matter what it pays. You must understand, however, that compensation discussions are a normal part of the employer-employee relationship. No question is out of scope when posed in a respectful manner.

It is natural for the employer and employee to discuss compensation, and to do so in a frank and honest manner. It is at this time in every hiring process where the niceties of recruiting are temporarily put aside, and the more hardcore compensation discussions take center stage. This is not when you want to appear timid or weak. Neither is it the time to be overly aggressive, ignorant, and demand a package that is totally out of line.

When discussions about remuneration are avoided today, issues about money are almost certain to bubble up to the surface in the future. This is because you did not clearly understand the position's total compensation package and your needs were not firmly established. This is most often due to a lack of nerve to directly address compensation at the appropriate time so that a full understanding is reached.

Companies are profit-based entities that expect to extract the most out of every dollar they invest in their people. This means they need to ensure they pay wages that are on par with, but not above, the norm. Many conduct surveys of comparable wages for the role in the geographical areas in which they do business. Others belong to wage and benefit information services, which offer this data for a fee. In both instances, access to data ensures employers know the top, bottom, and average wages for certain jobs in particular locales. Your challenge when in wage negotiations is to determine what that range is and where you fall within it. When you lack information about the range, ask about it so that you can make an informed decision based upon fact.

If you expect your employer to "take care of you" and treat you with maximum fairness with respect to compensation, you may be severely disappointed. Never trust that the company will take care of you with respect to the payment of a fair wage. This misplaced belief causes both parties issues in the future. You become unhappy, since your compensation may not match with your expectations. The company suffers, as they have a disgruntled employee. You must negotiate with your best interests in mind in this area, and secure a written offer that outlines exactly what you are to be paid. This is the same for a giant corporation as it is for a mom and pop enterprise. Just because an employer is small does not release them from the obligation to provide a written offer that defines compensation and benefits.

Financial discussions must be addressed with logic and without emotion. This is accomplished through thorough preparation and research. There is comparable salary and wage information on the internet that may be found via a simple search. There are also multiple sites that offer cost of living differentials between geographical areas. Use these as research tools in order to better understand the low, mid, and high points related to pay. Remember: these are general guidelines and should not be thought to be one hundred per cent reliable. Many internet-based information sources are not entirely accurate or up-to-date and should be used as a general guideline only. Your compensation target should also take experience and past performance into consideration.

Once you know your target number, you may now enter any financial negotiations with a calculated goal that permits a logical discussion to take place. It is imperative to write this number down. This written number should not be shared, but the act of writing it ingrains it in your mind. If you go begin negotiations without commitment to this target, it is all together possible that you may become emotionally unraveled during talks as you attempt to match an offer package with your needs. Logic and not emotions must rule your demeanor in pay-based talks. Some entry level jobs may not have any room for discussion. Other positions, especially those that are salary-based, typically have a range of pay that you should understand before you further progress through negotiations.

You must be prepared to walk away from an opportunity when it doesn't offer sufficient compensation to meet or exceed your pre-determined target. This is especially relevant if you are currently employed or otherwise not in desperate need of a job. This is one of the primary reasons you calculated this amount beforehand. It takes the emotion out of the equation and is insurance that you do not say "Yes" to something to which you should say "No, thanks."

Compensation negotiations most frequently take place in the context of an interview. These interviews have a flow. They may begin with a review of your background and move to a Question and Answer session where both you and the interviewer ask questions of each other. The guidance here is to compartmentalize the subject of compensation so it can be addressed at the proper time in the flow. You compartmentalize a topic when you isolate it from others during the course of a discussion. The topic's impact and emotional aspects are thereby contained and permit focus on it and it alone. The mention of the fact that you now wish to address compensation results in that topic becoming the discussion's focus. At the end of the compensation discussion, you and the interviewer should agree that dialog about compensation is complete and move on to your next topic.

POWERPOINT

NERVES ARE NATURAL

Everyone gets nervous in certain situations. This is a natural response when we are faced with an event that carries great importance or that may be perceived as threatening. Job interviews and salary negotiations certainly qualify.

Proper preparation for what is in front of you reduces nervousness in these situations. Make a list of possible interview questions, practice your elevator speech, and review your resume. Ensure how you link it to the job's requirements. Your focus on preparation reduces your stress level and makes you feel more confident.

Experience is a great teacher. After several interviews, you become more skilled and better able to convincingly relate your story. This is another reason why you should follow up on select job opportunities, since the interviews that come along with them offer the practice you need to excel. Your body of experience increases and you're your comfort level rises.

A certain amount of nervousness is natural, but it becomes more manageable with preparation and practice.

Respect your network

Personal networks require constant attention, care, and nurturing if they are to operate at their highest level. You should carefully build your own personal network and keep in periodic contact with its members so that when you may need to ask a favor, it is not viewed as an irregular activity and poorly received. Networks must be considered the gold standard of career development and treated as such.

You may reach out to others you know or have worked with in order to ask for referrals, references, and other assistance during a job search. This is as wise as it is common. You must understand that when you do this, you involve others in your search through your request for their active participation. In situations where an individual extends an offer to help you, it is a sign of respect that should not be taken lightly. Every such offer of assistance warrants an update regarding the progress of your job search. Anything less is disrespectful.

It is incumbent upon you to keep these networked supporters informed about the progress of your search. Do not demonstrate a lack of respect by your failure to update them after your initial request for help. When this happens, the result is that this network contact is lost along with any further benefit they may provide. It is maddening to assist someone, provide assistance, and then be left in the dark about the status of their search. The worst possible scenario is to land a new job, and not let the people who you asked to help know about your success.

A colleague's former employee called her to ask for assistance in his job search. She made several calls with personal contacts and set up promising introductions, but never heard from the former employee for several weeks. The reason was that he accepted another job offer and failed to inform his networking contact about his good fortune. As the bridge burned brightly in the background, she shared how disrespectful she believed his behavior to be, and that she would not extend any offer to help him again.

These hard feelings could have been avoided with a two minute phone call. Now, her former employee will no longer get her assistance in the future, and he has also turned a positive network contact into a negative. Not a smart career move.

It's how fast you produce

Prospective employers are not interested in whether or not you are a fast learner. They want to hire someone who produces at or near 100% capacity in the shortest time possible. They invest money in a new employee and they want a rapid return on that investment. That return is created when the employee executes the tasks associated with their job at a high enough level to offset the employer's investment. Employers want the fastest ramp time to full productivity from their new hires.

You need to communicate your understanding of this concept to prospective employers. Do not fall into the common trap that many candidates lay for themselves and say that you are a fast learner. This statement simply indicates that you are not qualified, and that you are most likely desperate for the job. Conversely, when you share how quickly you can become fully productive, you demonstrate that you understand how business works, and that you grasp the importance of a fast ramp up to full productivity.

Employers look to hire those who have the ability to contribute in the shortest period of time. They want to minimize their investment of money and time in new hires. This is a fact that is generally overlooked by those with little experience in the business world. It is not only limited to this segment of the work force, though. People with a higher level of experience often fall into this same trap.

To state that you are a fast learner is to say that you are desperate for a job. It screams that you are not qualified or experienced, but given a chance, you could probably provide sufficient return on investment to produce a benefit within some indeterminate time window. It is similar to a request for the employer to throw the dice in order to see if they produce a winner. The preferred way to demonstrate your qualifications for a prospective position is to offer to create a ninety day action plan. This plan outlines the steps that you will take within this timeframe to learn the job, ramp productivity, and begin to pay back the organization's investment in you. This does several things: it demonstrates you are serious about the position, it offers a glimpse into the application of your skills, and it methodically prompts the hiring agent to give you the opportunity to have a follow-on discussion about the job.

Unless a job opportunity states "On the Job Training," assume it requires that you must have the necessary background and experience in order to apply. Review the job description criteria then decide if you have enough points of intersection with the required competencies. This saves both you and the prospective employer time and energy.

READINESS REVIEW

This chapter touches on several very sensitive areas of everyone's life. What you do for a living does much to establish your identity, and has been called the world's window into who you are. It is common to pursue employment that is more in line with your goals and aspirations than the job you hold today. Change is natural. You may work at a job that is not particularly satisfying. These are frequently temporary in nature. They are either entry level roles or bridges to something better, since dissatisfaction is the great energizer for self-improvement. Once you receive your initial paycheck, you often find yourself in the hunt for something you believe is even more fulfilling.

It takes a specific skill set to be successful in your job searches. You need to view this skill set separately from your basic job requirements. It includes the items covered in this chapter as well as patience, perseverance, and a positive attitude. You would do well to learn this craft, since statistics do indicate that you will participate in multiple job searches over your career. Just as with your core skill set, the more you practice, the better you become. Your best first step is to learn what it is that you need to practice. Only then can you embark upon a logical, organized plan to improve your job search skills, and by doing so, improve your chances to secure better employment.

PERSONAL DEVELOPMENT ACTIONS

- Review your LinkedIn profile. Do you have one? Is it accurate and up to date? Does it accurately reflect your work history and skills? Review the profiles of successful individuals and determine what theirs may contain that yours does not. Update your profile accordingly. If you do not have a LinkedIn presence, create one.

- Perform a personal finance review. Do you have a savings plan, or do you live from paycheck to paycheck? Do you spend money on things that are not critical but that offer short term rewards? Make a decision to build a nest egg/war chest that can be used to see you through a period of unemployment. Write the plan down and review it each payday until it becomes automatic.

- Write your personal elevator speech. Does it state who you are personally and professionally within fifteen to thirty seconds? Can you say it easily and with conviction and without notes? Take the time to write your elevator speech and learn to speak it with ease. You will find it useful in many different situations.

- Read a book, article, or paper on negotiation skills. Have you been in a situation where you had to negotiate salary or other job-related element? Would you have been better prepared if you were aware of the basics of successful negotiations? Awareness of this skill provides an edge in multiple areas of your professional life.

- Calculate how much it costs an organization to recruit and hire for a new position. Are you aware of the different cost associated with the addition of a new job? List the costs associated with advertising, travel, Human Resources personnel, interviews, training, and low performance normally attributed to a new employee despite the fact they receive their full pay. Can you see the impact you can make on the hiring manager by stating that you will quickly return their investment in you vs. saying that you are a fast learner? Your awareness of this investment gives you an edge that could make the difference in a hiring decision.

EPILOGUE

Your personal definition of success evolves over the course of your career as you mature and as your views and values change. What you consider successful today may change drastically at different points in the future. What is important is that you clearly know your current definition, so you have a specific target to work towards. When you move along your career path, you measure yourself against your definition of success on an ongoing basis in order to determine your progress towards your personal goals. In the process, there are several things that should not be forgotten:

- Don't be in too much of a hurry. Success is built much like a wall ... one brick at time. It is okay if you are not a Vice President by the age of twenty-five. Give yourself time to mature, season, and age. Enjoy the journey. As was mentioned earlier, focus on the work and the prize follows.

- Unwaveringly adhere to your core values. Little else is more important than this. In order to adhere to your values, you must be able to define them. If you are not clear what they are at this point, I suggest you immediately do the work necessary to find out.

- Look beyond the material aspect of everything. There is more to life than what is found in the material realm. While it should definitely not be ignored, your material side can derail both you and your career, if not held in check.

This book is designed to make you think about a wide range of topics, and not just provide "10 Easy Steps to Success." Those easy steps do not exist. A successful career is the sum of diligent, thoughtful work, which is executed over an extended period of time. It is a blend of skill, knowledge, experience, and attitude mixed with self-promotion, collaboration, discipline, and networking. It requires a healthy dose of skepticism about what you hear from others, regardless of their position. It is a pursuit that constantly demands that you balance your business life with your personal life, so that one does not control the other. Career success also contains elements of luck. Luck can be defined as success by happenstance, but that is much too general. Good luck happens more to people who prepare themselves appropriately. It occurs when individuals pay attention to details, educate themselves, and minimize those factors in their lives that could negatively impact their opportunities for success. Those who have less good luck than what they believe they should experience are usually members of the group that is ill prepared and less willing to put in the hard work. The equation is simple: in order to get your fair share of return, you have to put in your fair share of work. Entitlement is not a factor in the equation.

This book was created as a way to share my experiences with my daughters who are both in the early stages of their careers. I soon realized that what I share with them would also put many of these same things into perspective for other readers as well. My goal for them as well as you is to generate thoughts and resulting actions about a wide variety of topics and how they may relate to you (and you to them). The points of view are based upon real life situations that I observed, experienced, and noted. There are examples for many of the items that are covered. I feel you only have to open your eyes to see other examples all around you.

Your next step, should you decide to take it, is to choose to make a difference. When you make a difference in your work life, change happens in your personal life. That interplay between the two is important to recognize. This book is meant to improve your life at work, reduce the surprises that you face there, and make travel on your personal career path more efficient and rewarding. The fact that you chose to read *Eyes Open Employment* was Step One. Now, the challenge is to take the Next Step and put it into action.